聽說長洲

CHEUNG CHAU TELLS

兩代

藝

Legacy

Crafts

序

香港人說「入長洲」，長洲人說「出香港」，一出一入，雖然只是五十分鐘船程，卻彷彿是兩個國度，兩種生活——島的，和城市的。

長洲可算是全香港 261 個離島之中，最為香港人所熟悉的一個。誰都知道，那裡有大魚蛋、糯米糍和平安包，有烙印了很多人的青春回憶的海灘，有著名海盜張保仔的寶洞。然而，真正定義這小島的性格特質和內涵的，往往是藏在景點背後那些不能輕易被消費的東西。

《號外》雜誌的創辦人丘世文的父親丘東明曾著《一九二零年代長洲生活記趣》一書，是坊間少有書寫長洲的個人回憶錄。他筆下的長洲落後、腥臭、陌生，在長洲生活的幾年，可說是他的童年陰影，唯有北帝廟和東灣沙灘為他一解少年愁苦。一百年後的今日，北帝廟前的海填了，漁業式微了，但島上仍然保留不少傳統的工業、手藝和信仰習俗，同時間，許多島二、三代，以至城市人選擇搬到島上居住和創業，在長洲開拓更多生活的可能性。本書分為漁、食、兩代和藝四部分，呈現長洲的新舊交融，以及不同人的堅持與掙扎。

長洲有句俗語，說人人都是「水流柴」，意指大家都是從五湖四海來到此地，像漂到沙灘上的木頭。長洲是雜姓島，早期大部分人口為來自內地不同城市的漁民，逐漸發展成以漁鹽業為主的重要墟市，《新安縣志》提到長洲「在急水門外，大奚山（即大嶼山）南，長十餘里，商賈多聚集於此」。一如香港曾經也是個「借來的地方」，幾代下來，過客終落地生根，陌生的土地就成了「我城」，成了國際大都會。長洲，彷如香港的縮影。長洲人的故事，也是香港人的故事。

本書訪問了 25 位不同行業、年齡和身分的長洲人，聽他們訴說長洲的歷史、文化、生活方式和故事。對於這居住了二萬多人的島，本書所涵蓋的只是冰山一角，只望以此為起點，讓讀者看見長洲的不同面貌。

Foreword

Those living in Hong Kong would say they are "visiting Cheung Chau", while Cheung Chau islanders always say they are "heading to Hong Kong" whenever they go to town. Though only a 50-minute ferry ride apart, it seems to suggest the two ways of living: the island's and the city's.

Cheung Chau may very well be Hongkongers' most familiar island out of the city's 261 outlying islands. Everyone knows of its large fish balls, mango mochis and Ping On buns. The island's beaches also hold a special place in many people's youthful memories, not to mention its treasure cave of the infamous pirate Cheung Po Tsai. Yet what truly defines this island is not something that can be commodified.

Yau Tung Ming—father of Joseph Yau, a co-founder of City Magazine—wrote a memoir called *Down and Out in Cheung Chau, 1920s* inspired by the island. In his account, Cheung Chau was a backward and putrid place. The Pak Tai Temple and Tung Wan Beach were his only places of refuge during the few years of his unpleasant stay.

Now a century later, the harbourfront of Pak Tai Temple has been reclaimed and the island's fishing industry has dwindled. But many traditional industries, crafts and religious customs have managed to live on. Meanwhile, many second and third generations of Cheung Chau natives, as well as city dwellers who have moved to the island, choose to launch new businesses to experiment with the many possibilities of living on Cheung Chau.

Each of the four sections of this book—fishery, delicacies, legacy, crafts—reveals the melding of the new and the old on Cheung Chau, as well as the perseverance and struggles of the islanders.

A expression from Cheung Chau says that everyone is a *sui lau chai* (literally "wood floating on water"), meaning everyone has arrived at this land from all corners of the world, just like a piece of wood that has drifted ashore. The residents of Cheung Chau are not from a single clan. Most of its earliest dwellers were fishermen from different cities, who have developed the island into an important fishing and salt-making port.

Cheung Chau and Hong Kong are very much alike: once a borrowed place, in which former drifters have settled down and taken roots after several generations. The stories of Cheung Chau-ers are indeed those of Hongkongers.

This book includes 25 interviews with Cheung Chau-ers of different occupations, ages and positions, each telling their tales of the island's history, culture, way of life. For an island with a population of over 20,000, what this book can cover is only the tip of an iceberg. The two-year interview period coincided with the outbreak of a global epidemic. Facing unprecedented uncertainties, the interviewees and Hong Kong have gone through numerous changes.

We hope this book can serve as a starting point for you to take a sneak peek at the many faces of Cheung Chau at this particular time and space.

人 *People*

居民連漁民流動人口約二萬餘人。2006及2016的《中期人口普查》均顯示，長洲為人煙最稠密的離島。

Cheung Chau has a total population of about 20,000, which includes residents and a floating population of fishermen. The 2006 and 2016 Population By-censuses both show that Cheung Chau is the most populated outlying island.

地 *Land*

位於香港島以外約16公里的西南海域，東南方為大嶼山、北望喜靈洲。小島面積約2.46平方公里，在全港離島區中排名第五。由南、北兩個高約百米的小丘，並由連接兩者之間的一條狹長的沖積平原所構成。

Cheung Chau is located in the seas about 16 km southwest of Hong Kong Island, with Lantau Island in its southeast, and it looks north at Hei Ling Chau. The island covers an area of about 2.46 km^2, ranking Cheung Chau the fifth largest island within the Islands District. It is composed of two 100-metre hills in the north and the south, connected by a long and narrow alluvial plain.

水 *Water*

食水來自大嶼山銀鑛灣濾水廠，是極少數非依賴中國東江水的地區。

舊時居民和商戶須到公眾水井取水，或向私營水艇買水。直至1955年，政府從大嶼山拾塱附近的儲水池，接駁一條海底輸水管，至長洲大貴灣山頭的貯水庫，長洲才有自來水供應。

The drinking water on Cheung Chau comes from the Silver Mine Bay Water Treatment Works on Lantau Island, which is one of the very few areas that does not depend on imported water supply from China.

In the old days, residents and merchants had to either fetch water from public wells, or buy water from private water boats. Cheung Chau had no running water supply until 1955, when the government built a submarine water pipe that connected the storage tank near Shap Long on Lantau Island to the reservoir at the top of Tai Kwai Wan.

長洲原本是兩個島

Cheung Chau Was Two Separate Islands

很多人稱長洲為「啞鈴島」，因其地勢狹長，兩邊闊，中間窄，呈「工」字型，又似啞鈴。原來長洲是個連島沙洲，從前是兩個分開的島，但因受島嶼的形狀以及季候風的影響，冬天吹東北風，夏天吹東南風，令到沙泥在南北兩島的沿岸堆積，經年累月兩島最終連成一線，現時島上最熱鬧的東灣泳灘和海傍街，都是建在沙洲上。

Cheung Chau is known as the "Dumbbell Island" because of its long and narrow terrain, which is wide on both sides and narrow in the middle. The shape resembles the Chinese character of *gong*.

Now a tombolo, Cheung Chau used to be two separate islands. However, due to the shape of the islands and effects of monsoons, the sand accumulated along the coasts of the two islands and they gradually became one. Nowadays, the most popular Tung Wan Beach and Pak She Praya Road were both built on the sandbank.

平安包

Ping On Bun

太平清醮包山上的包子，均由超渡亡魂用的「幽包」砌成。島民認為吃過印上朱紅色的「福」、「安」、「壽」等吉祥字樣的包子能保平安，因此稱為「平安包」。軟糯雪白的蒸包內藏蓮蓉、豆沙或蔴蓉等口味。每次儀式結束後，均見不少市民排隊購買平安包，祈求家人平安。

平安包現為當之無愧的長洲名物，這白底紅字的小小包子更為小島帶來龐大商機。紀念品店全年售賣平安包的衍生產品，如鑰匙扣、磁石、飾物等等。近年一些傳統麵包店更銳意革新，與不同年輕品牌合作，推出印有卡通人物和電影角色造型的平安包及禮盒。

The "Bun Mountains" at the Cheung Chau Bun Festival are made up of "netherworld buns" that are used to guide the spirits of the dead. Islanders believe that eating these buns with auspicious Chinese characters such as *fuk* (good fortune), *on* (safety) and *sau* (longevity) stamped in red can keep them safe (*ping on*), hence the name "Ping On" bun. These pillowy steamed buns are each filled with lotus, red bean or sesame paste. At the end of each ceremony, many citizens line up to buy Ping On buns in prayer for their families' safety.

Ping On buns even bring huge business opportunities to the island. Souvenir shops sell Ping On bun-inspired merchandise such as keychains and fridge magnets all year round. Recent years have seen more crossovers between traditional bakeries and young brands, producing Ping On buns and gift boxes printed with cartoon and movie characters.

不是長洲的長洲大魚蛋？

Are Cheung Chau Big Fish Balls from Cheung Chau?

如乒乓球大小的大魚蛋，不少人認為是源於長洲。不過，長洲街坊普遍對此嗤之以鼻，那到底大魚蛋從何而來？大魚蛋的出現眾說紛紜，綜合一眾漁民及街坊說法，2003年沙士肆虐後旅遊業一落千丈，唯有各出其謀，有店舖想出用巨大化魚蛋作噱頭，大大粒的魚蛋旋即成遊客的合照寵兒，漸漸才成為長洲名物。

大魚蛋多出產自新加坡和中國，主要成份為澱粉和魚味粉。來貨成本極低，加上只需數個電池爐的低度經營，厚利多銷，吸引愈來愈多店舖以此作招徠。為了突圍而出，店舖會提供多種醬汁選擇，除了常見的咖哩和沙嗲，還有較新穎的麻辣和梅汁口味。

目前，島上的手打魚蛋店只餘寥寥數間。店家天未亮便把門鱔或九棍等鮮魚去皮拆肉、反覆打至起膠成魚漿，再唧出一粒粒魚蛋。如指頭大的小丸子當然不如大魚蛋般飽足，但名符其實魚蛋有魚味，所以即使多年來不斷漲價，仍不乏捧場客。

Many people believe the big fish ball, with the size of a ping pong ball, to be from Cheung Chau. However, Cheung Chau locals tend to turn their noses up at it.

Then where does the big fish ball come from? There are different sayings about its origins. According to some fishermen and kaifongs, after the raging of SARS in 2003, businesses had to come up with creative strategies and gimmicks to attract tourists. The photogenic gigantified fish balls soon became a tourist favourite and subsequently a Cheung Chau specialty.

Big fish balls—made of starch and fish powder—are mostly produced in Singapore and China. Cheap ingredients and extremely simple cooking have convinced more and more shops to sell it.

To stand out, some shops provide a wide selection of sauces, from the commonly found curry and satay sauces to newer flavours like mala and plum.

Nowadays, there are only very few handmade fish ball shops left on Cheung Chau. After deboning and skinning fresh fish such as conger-pike eel and whiting, shopkeepers need to repeatedly beat the flesh into a fish paste, then squeeze it into balls. These thumb-sized fish balls are of course not as filling as the big ones, but they carry the authentic flavour of fish. These smaller handmade balls have attracted many loyal fans over the years, despite the constantly hiking prices.

全港最後一個關閉的信號站

The Last Signal Station to Close in Hong Kong

在電台、電視、手機未普及之前，天文台要向市民發出風暴消息，就要靠全港四十多個信號站，懸掛起實體「風球」(熱帶氣旋警告信號)，但由於其後有更快捷方便的方法獲得風暴消息，信號站於七十年代起逐漸關閉，而位於長洲的信號站，是全港最後一個關閉的，於 2002 年 1 月 1 日才停用。根據香港天文台的資料，長洲信號站於 1962 年設於當時碼頭附近的警署內，至 1971 年遷至位於近關公忠義亭的山頭的氣象站內。資料又指，以前在長洲工作的科學助理，每次當值都連踩九日，夜闌人靜可觀星賞月，日頭又可去東灣游泳、到長洲戲院看電影、去碼頭食海鮮，聽上去算是份優差。信號站多年間掛起過無數風球，單是十號風球便掛過五次，最嚴峻的一次莫過於 1983 年「愛倫」襲港，信號站內懸掛風球的桅桿也遭吹彎。

Before the prevalence of radio, television and mobile phones, the observatory needed to spread the news of storms by displaying visual signals at over 40 signal stations across Hong Kong. However, signal stations started to close down in the 1970s when quicker ways to broadcast information became available.

The signal station on Cheung Chau was the last to close in Hong Kong, only halting operations on 1 January 2002. According to the Hong Kong Observatory, the Cheung Chau signal station was originally situated within the police station near the pier in 1962, before it was moved to a hilltop near the Kwan Kung Pavilion in 1971. Scientific assistants working on Cheung Chau back then would work for nine days straight every shift. In the night they could watch the moon and the stars; during the day they could swim in Tung Wan or go to movies at the Cheung Chau Theatre.

The signal station had hoisted numerous typhoon signals over the years—signal no. 10 alone was hoisted five times. The worst one was in 1983 when Typhoon Ellen hit Hong Kong, even the station's mast was bent.

Chapter 01

第一章

Fishery

漁

古時的香港以漁村起家，據鹽田遺址和出土文物顯示，捕魚活動可上溯至石器時代，更是十九世紀開埠初期時的主要經濟支柱，60年代初錄得高達超過一萬艘漁船，直到千禧年代才逐漸萎縮，下降至現時的約五千艘。

被譽為「香港八大漁港」之一的長洲，早在明清時期漁業非常繁盛，50年代島上更有近二萬名漁民，至今西灣北村外的海面仍有不少漁船停泊，多年來見證本地漁業的興衰。漁船大多數由水上家庭世代相傳，早年多是一家老幼擠在一隻小小住家艇上捕魚和起居飲食，直至60年代才陸續搬到岸上。漁業亦衍生了不少附屬工業，漁網漁具、建船修艇、餐飲海味、製冰等等，養活了世世代代的島民。

現在，我們一起看看，水上人二三代人所面對的生活和變遷，還有歷史悠久的長洲捕漁業文化。

The history of Hong Kong began with fishing villages. Evident in the Yim Tin archaeological site and artefacts, local fishing activities could be dated back to the Stone Age and had been central to the economy in the 19th century. Hong Kong's fishing industry began to peak in the early 1960s, boasting over 10,000 fishing boats. The number gradually declined at the turn of the 21st century and only around 5,000 are left today.

Known as one of Hong Kong's eight major fishing harbours, Cheung Chau was home to approximately 20,000 fishermen during the 50s. Today, quite a few fishing boats can still be seen around the bay of Sai Wan. They are largely passed down from generation to generation among boat dwellers. Large families used to live and pursue their livelihood of fishing on the sea. It was not until the 60s that boat people gradually moved into regular housings onshore.

The fishing business has also given birth to many subsidiary industries such as boat construction and repairs, ice-making, the sales of fishing tools, seafood eateries, and dried seafood... all of which would go on to feed generations of islanders.

In this chapter, we set sail into the changing landscape and unique cultural heritage of Cheung Chau's fishing industry.

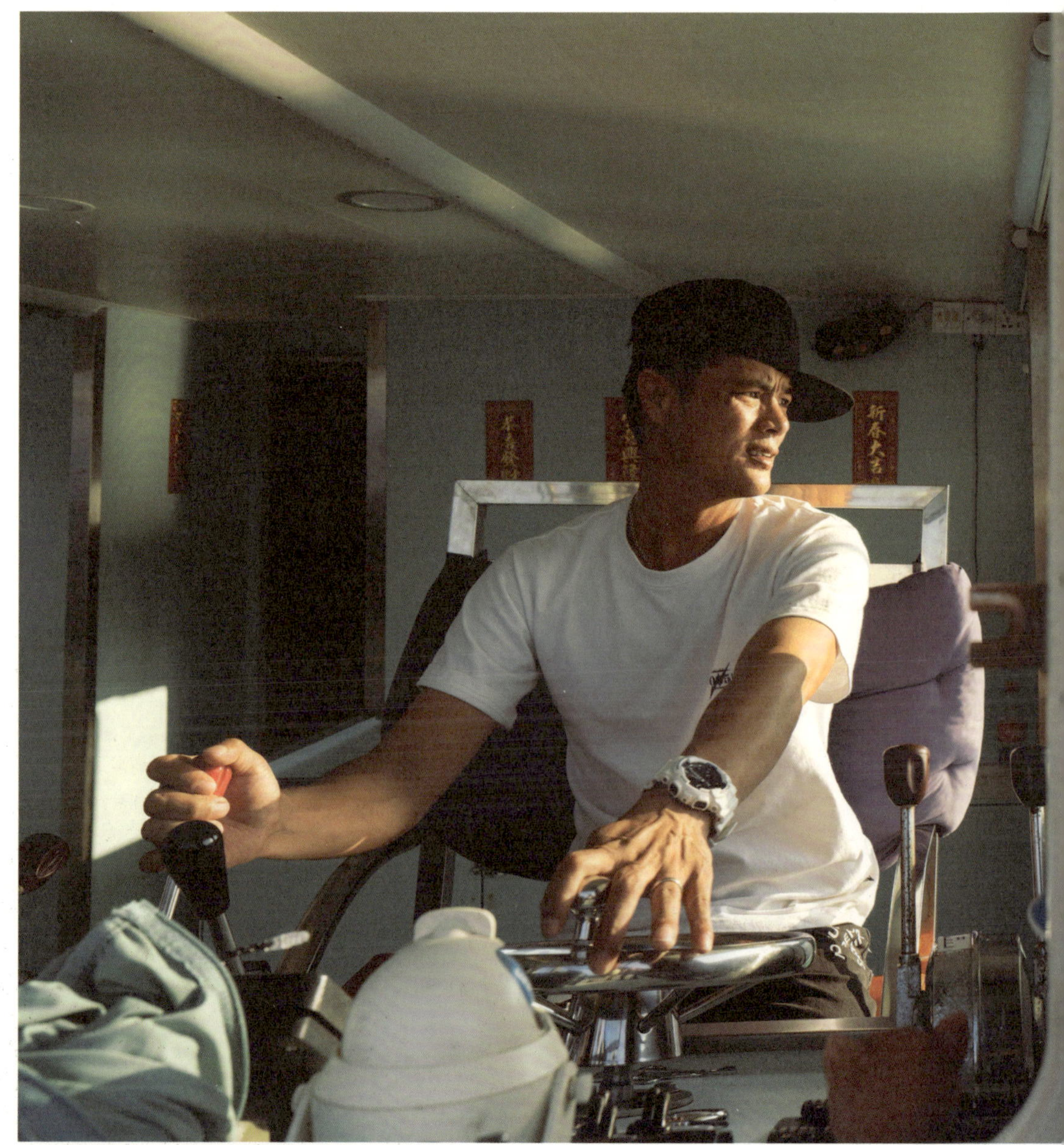
新春大吉

第三代漁民阿強

A Third-Generation Fisherman

第三代漁民阿強
見證本地漁業起落

人稱阿強的羅少強年約四十多歲，算得上是整個長洲第二年輕的船東，視捕魚為終生職業。

「做這一行，沒特別話好或不好啦。我自細跟爸爸出海捉魚，讀書不多，即使上岸都是做辛苦工。」他二十多歲時曾出香港從事地盤工作，三十五歲因父親退休才回到長洲出海作業，後來大哥和兩位弟弟相繼加入，便賣掉父親的漁船，購入兩艘更耐用的玻璃纖維船。「現在既然揸船捉魚都算搵到錢，都預會做到老。」

阿強祖籍廣東寶安，爺爺是芝麻灣十塱村的漁民。阿強的父親說：「我小時住艇，沒有書讀，十幾歲就開始跟我伯爺工作。舊式漁船邊有引擎丫！每天出海都要人手搖櫓，又要靠眼望要不要落網，捉完魚又要補網織網。以前捉魚真的辛苦多了，沒有手套戴又沒有鞋穿，在船上生活只得一個篷篷遮風擋雨，常常冷到睡不著。」加上以往的天氣預報遠不如現今準確，漁民不時要抬頭留意著天氣狀態，真正見風駛悝。

阿強的父親多年來靠海而活，因孩子要上學便搬到長洲灣，三十年前買樓搬到岸上居住，直至七八年前才退休。「現在四個仔、一個女、九個孫，全都在長洲，梗係開心囉！上街（退休上岸）後沒什麼不習慣，閒時也會跟他們出去看看，坐坐船。」

身為第三代漁民，阿強同樣見證著香港捕漁業的種種變遷。自 2012 年底起，香港政府禁止漁民在本地水域進行拖網捕魚。「摻繒[1]等拖網漁船殺傷力很大，等於把漁網伸到海牀，無差別地刮起底層棲息的生物。但圍網有得揀，影響範圍始終較細。」阿強記得那時一下子少了很多大船出沒，反而漸漸多了舢舨和捉蝦為主的「打網仔[2]」。

阿強的「小露寶號」為長約七十呎的罟仔艇，還拖著一隻小艇，用作拉著漁網繞一個圈圍捕。至於被問到漁船何以取名，阿強笑著搔搔頭：「其實是因

[1] 採用摻繒作業的漁民，會在船舷兩旁特設的木撐架上懸掛長網袋，捕撈在近水面層棲息的魚蝦。

[2]「打網仔」又稱「敲魚」，漁民先佈置好漁網，再用長柄大鎚敲打魚網附近水面。受驚亂竄的魚兒，很容易便會撞上魚網，不能逃脫。

為自小街坊都是叫我『小露寶』，叫著叫著就連船都用上這個名號。」跟不少漁民一樣，阿強會在船尾上香，祈求風調雨順，另又掛著一柄掃把，傳說可擋去龍捲風。

小露寶號持兩地牌，可在香港和內地水域作業。但即使近岸的捕魚量不如遠洋般高，阿強也從未想過轉投深海作業。「遠洋好辛苦，成日都上唔到岸。住長洲最好就是可以隨時約朋友見面吹水，近岸捉魚至少每天都可以返來。」他多數去鄰近長洲的大嶼山、南丫島附近捕魚，「最遠就是去大澳，都要至少一小時。」

阿強僱了八名駐船內地漁工，住在船的下層，上下床位以掛簾間隔。八人捕魚前後甚少交談，卻默契十足，原來全來自同一條村。1995 年漁護署與入境處合作引入內地漁工，以紓緩本地業界人手短缺的問題。而長洲的內地漁工多來自廣東省的電白區和遂溪，由於入境管制規定他們不得離船，起居飲食全在船上進行。阿強會替他們到街市買菜，又會每月額外給予伙食津貼，閒時和他們一起吃飯喝啤酒，落力和伙記們打成一片。「始終他們要離鄉別井，聯誼一下也不錯啦。」內地漁工每年都只在農曆新年才回鄉與家人團聚，疫情下更是歸鄉無期。

中港兩地日漸緊密的聯繫，除了改寫了從事捕漁的人口結構，還帶動市場供求的變化。「以前捉魚只供香港市場，一件餅仔分不了多少人。但七八年前大陸開放，開始食得起鹹水魚，不再只食鯇魚。市場一下子大了，不單魚價高了，還要捉幾多便賣幾多。」阿強每次出海捕魚後，便會通知相熟批發商，一般會約在兩地水域交界進行交收，漁獲多分銷到珠海等地。

上層的駕駛座前有數個屏幕，除了顯示礁石分佈的雷達導航，還有一個探魚儀。不過阿強自幼跟父親出海，也習慣用肉眼觀察。夕陽下的海面波光粼粼，但外行人根本看不到任何魚蹤。阿強笑言：「始終我出海出了那麼多年。平靜如鏡時會比較容易留意到它們躍出水的蹤跡，現在有浪會比較難看到，就可以留意附近有沒有鳥類盤旋。」漁民和海鳥有著相互依存的關係，每次撒網，爭相躍出水面的魚兒即引來一群海鷗覓食。

「今日比較大風，多數都不會有很多魚。」他又指指數百米內的三四架漁船，「你看看，大家都是圍在這區，我大表哥的船都在。」僧多粥少，當然會影

響漁獲，但阿強倒是既來之則安之，還興致勃勃用無線電對講機與不遠處的表哥閒聊。

入夜後阿強繼續駕著船在芝麻灣、喜靈洲、大白灣（又稱愉景灣）一帶徘徊，不時拿起駕駛座旁的大光燈照射海面，察看有沒有魚群聚集之餘，亦可吸引游魚。途經大嶼山的長沙灣時他指著海魚養殖區介紹：「長洲和香港仔出售的海魚，九成九都是來自這個魚排。」原來阿強的父親亦曾沾手養魚業。「以前在芝麻灣養魚養過廿幾年，不過之後我們都不想打理，就賣了給別人。」

阿強鎖定目標魚群後，就會跟下層的內地漁工溝通。兩名漁工就會駕著小艇，快速圓弧形航行放網，形成包圍圈，同時母船上的船員會不停用水舂擊打水面，迫使魚群進入網囊。當小艇回到母船旁邊，便會交接網具並固定於船首的絞網機，收緊網底後把網拉起，再由船員用抄網撈出漁獲。「現在有起網機，用機器把網絞上來，又有大陸漁民幫手，快捷和省力得多。以前我們得四兄弟一齊揸船，又要人手拉網，當然差好遠。」

雖然船員衣穿防水連身褲，配著斗笠帽、膠手袖和勞工手套，包得密不透風，但每次收網後總會拿水喉洗臉和沖身。然後便會按魚的品種和大小分類，再加冰雪冷凍儲存。經分類後，大量黃魚和鰽魚倒進橙色大膠箱，每個長方形箱的容量達一百五十斤。另有兩三尾黃花魚、鷹鯧就用小篩籃分開存放。「黃花這些可以賣多幾十倍價錢，較矜貴。最細的魚尾就賣給魚排餵魚餵蟹。」出海當晚第二次落網就在長洲東灣對出，撈上來的漁獲卻夾著一大堆白鮓（即水母），員工要逐一撈出再拋回海裡。「天氣熱令水變暖，白鮓就會成群冒出來。聽說以前的漁民會任由它們擱在甲板上，太陽一曬就自然會化成水。」

當晚下午四時出海，直至約晚上九時才回島，五小時內圍網三次，共得六擔魚，即約六百斤，收獲不算豐富。阿強表示：「有時會打到二百擔，不過我們靠天吃飯，怎說得準呢。」

漁民除了無法左右天氣，對人為填海亦只能無奈接受。對明日大嶼等對海洋生態有莫大影響的工程，阿強坦言沒法預計對附近一帶水域的影響。他說：「起港珠澳大橋時，少了很多不同種類的魚在這兒水域出沒，所以之後再有大型填海工程，或多或少總有影響，都無辦法。」

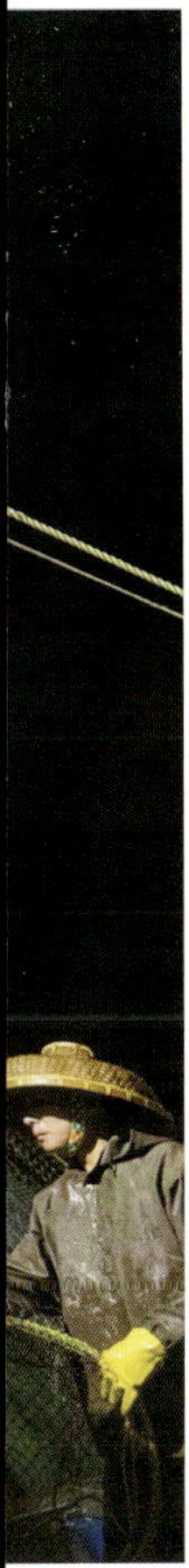

A Day in the Life of **A THIRD-GENERATION FISHERMAN**

Now in his early 40s, Keung is probably the second youngest vessel owner on Cheung Chau. To him, fishing is a lifelong occupation. "There's nothing particularly good or bad about this work," says Keung. "I started helping out on my father's boat from a young age. With my level of education, I wouldn't have many choices apart from physical labour if I moved to Hong Kong." After having spent his 20s in the city for construction work, Keung returned to Cheung Chau at the age of 35 to take the helm from his retiring father. As his three brothers joined the operation, he sold his father's boat and acquired two more durable fiberglass vessels. "Since I can make a living from fishing, I plan to do it until I retire."

Keung's family hails from Bao'an, Guangdong; his grandfather was a fisherman from Chi Ma Wan's Shap Long Village. Keung's father says, "I grew up on a boat without going to school, and started working with my uncle in my teens." There weren't engines on old fishing boats back then. Keung's father and grandfather had to oar manually each day and decide where to cast their nets by sight. After fishing, they often mended and made new nets before they could call it a day.

"It was a lot tougher back then. We didn't have gloves or shoes or a proper shelter over our heads. It was so cold that I often couldn't sleep," the second-generation fisherman recalls. Also because weather forecasts used to be less accurate, fishermen were obliged to pay close attention to weather conditions, which dictated their every move.

Keung's father had lived on the sea for decades. He moved to Cheung Chau Wan when his children started going to school. It was not until around 30 years ago that he bought a brick-and-mortar home on the island, where he retired around eight years ago. "I now have four sons, a daughter, and nine grandchildren, all on Cheung Chau—of course I'm happy!" Keung's father says he has adjusted quite well to retirement. "I still go on boat trips and outings with my family occasionally."

As a third-generation fisherman, Keung has experienced various changes in Hong Kong's fishing industry. In 2012, the Hong Kong government banned trawl fishing in local waters. "Hang trawling[1] is greatly destructive.

They extend netting to the seabed and scrape up creatures dwelling in the bottom indiscriminately," he explains. "With purse seining, you get to choose what species to catch and limit impacted areas." Following the ban, there was a sudden drop in the number of large vessels, which have since been gradually replaced by sampans and shrimp boats.

Keung's *Robocon* is a 70-foot-long vessel. It has a sampan in tow, which encircles fish with a net. Keung explains the name with a sheepish grin: "My neighbours had been calling me Robocon since I was a child. The nickname followed me throughout the years and became the boat's name." Like many fishermen, Keung burns incense at the tail of the boat in prayer for favourable weather. He also keeps a hanging broom in the hope to ward off cyclones.

With *Robocon*'s license, Keung can operate in both Hong Kong and Mainland waters. Despite the lower yield near shore compared with that of far seas, Keung never considers pivoting to deep sea operation. "Deep sea fishing is rough. You spend little time onshore. The best thing about being on Cheung Chau is that I can meet up with friends any time. By fishing near shore, at least I can return to the island every day." He generally works near the neighbouring Lantau Island and Lamma Island. "The furthest I go is to Tai O. It takes at least one hour."

Keung has a team of eight live-in crew members from Mainland China. They live on the lower deck, sleeping in bunks separated by curtains. All from the same village, they cooperate seamlessly throughout the fishing operation without talking much.

In 1995, the government started bringing in fishing workers from the Mainland as a solution to the local labour shortage. They are mostly from Dianbai and Suixi in Guangdong. Since the immigration law bars them from leaving their vessels, Keung often runs to the wet market to get groceries for them. Besides extra monthly food allowances, he shares meals and

1 The long large cone-shaped nets are hung on a wood frame over the side of the vessel, extending just below the bottom to catch fishes and shrimps that are near the water surface.

beers with them in his spare time. “They are all far from home after all. It‘s always good to hang out and have fun together.” As these workers can only visit their families during Lunar New Year, their homebound trips have been indefinitely delayed during the pandemic.

With the Mainland and Hong Kong growing closer, the demography of the fishing population is not the only thing that has changed. Supply and demand in the market have also undergone massive shifts. “Previously, our fish was only for the local market, so profits were limited,” he notes. “However, since the Mainland‘s opening up seven or eight years ago, people who used to only buy grass carp could gradually afford saltwater fish. Thanks to the expanded market, fish prices have spiked, and we now sell everything we catch.” After every fishing trip, he contacts regular wholesalers to make trade, generally at China and Hong Kong‘s intersecting waters. The catch is mostly sold to places such as Zhuhai.

At the captain‘s seat on the upper deck, there are several screens displaying radar graphics of reef distribution and shoal detection. But having been out on the sea with his father since childhood, Keung is used to observing with the naked eye. Looking at sea waves glimmering under the sunset, no trace of any fish seems to be in sight.

“I’ve been on the sea for so many years after all. When the surface is perfectly still, it’s easier to spot fish jumping out of the water.” He adds, “It’s harder to see with the waves right now, so we can pay attention to the birds hovering nearby.” The relationship between fishermen and sea birds is symbiotic—every time a net is cast, a flock of seagulls is instantly attracted by the leaping fish.

“It‘s a windy day. We‘ll likely not get a large yield.” Keung points at the three or four fishing vessels within a few hundred metres. “Look, everyone is here. And that’s my cousin‘s boat.” Competition no doubt affects his harvest, but it does not bother Keung, who is thrilled to catch up with his cousin over the walkie-talkie.

After nightfall, Keung continues to sail along the areas of Chi Ma Wan, Hei Ling Chau, and Tai Pak Wan (a.k.a. Discovery Bay). He occasionally flashes

a floodlight at the water, a gesture that enables him to find shoals and attract fish. As he passes by Lantau Island's Cheung Sha Wan, he points at the marine fish culture area: "99% of marine fish sold on Cheung Chau and Hong Kong Island are from here." Keung's father had once engaged in fish farming. "He had a fish farm in Chi Ma Wan for 20-odd years, but none of us wanted to maintain it, so we sold the farm."

Once Keung targets a shoal, he communicates with his crew in the lower deck. Two of them quickly drive the sampan in an arc while casting net to create a circular trap. Meanwhile, the main vessel crew hits the water repeatedly with a pump-like tool, which forces the shoal into the net. As the sampan returns to the main vessel's side, they hand over the net and secure it to a net roller, then tighten the base and roll it up. The catch is retrieved with a dip net. "Now that we have a net roller and the help from Mainland fishermen, the process is much more efficient." He compares, "It used to be just my three brothers and me manning the vessel and pulling up nets by hand, which was of course entirely different."

Even though crew members are completely covered in waterproof overalls, bamboo hats, plastic sleeves, and work gloves, they always hose themselves down after each catch. Fish is sorted by species and size, after which a large amount of small yellow croakers and long-tailed anchovies are poured into a large plastic orange box filled with ice. Each rectangular box can hold up to 150 catties, or 75 kilograms.

Separated in small sieve baskets are a few large yellow croakers and Chinese silver pomfrets. "Large yellow croakers are more valuable," Keung explains. "They can be sold at least ten times more expensive than the small ones. Smaller fishes are usually sold to fish farms as fish and crab feed."

The second catch near Cheung Chau's Tung Wan is filled with jellyfish, which amass in hot weather. "Legend has it that fishermen used to simply leave them on the deck, where they melt into water under sunlight." But workers on Keung's vessel anyway scoop them up and toss them back to the sea one by one.

Having been out since 4 p.m., the crew returns at 9 p.m. The three catches in five hours have yielded six *tam*—a relatively small catch of 300 kilograms. Keung says, “Sometimes we get 200 tam, but it all depends on the weather.”

Weather aside, also beyond fishermen’s control is reclamation. Speaking of construction projects that can suffocate marine life such as the Lantau Tomorrow project, Keung confesses there is no way to predict what may happen to the nearby waters. “When they built the Hong Kong-Zhuhai-Macao Bridge, we saw a huge drop in fish species in the area,” the veteran fisherman recounts. “Any future large-scale reclamation project is bound to affect the waters one way or another. And there’s nothing we can do about it.”

本地捕撈漁船

LOCAL FISHING VESSELS

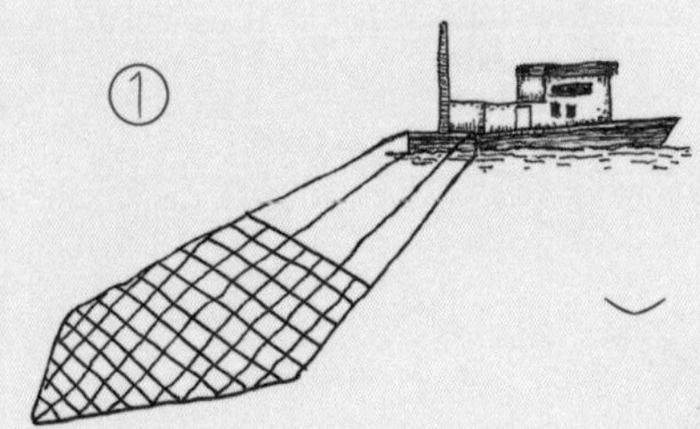
①

香港的漁船大多爲家庭式營運，
而且世代相傳。主要的捕魚方法包括各類拖網、
延繩釣、刺網、圍網／罟網、手釣及浸籠。

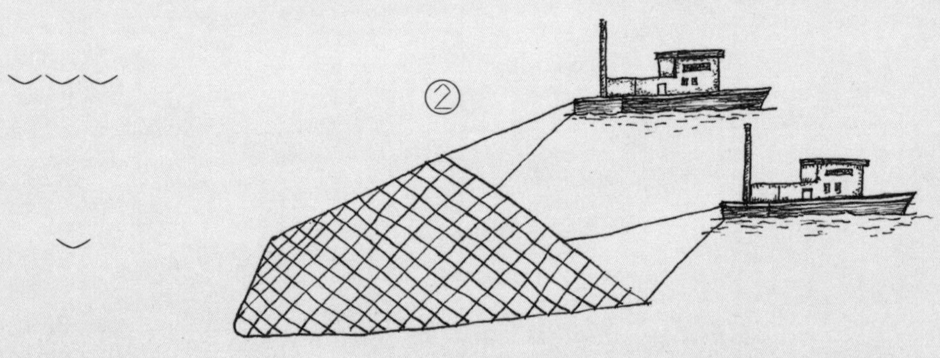
②

Hong Kong's fishing vessels are mostly run as family businesses handed down from one generation to another.

Main fishing methods include different types of trawling, long lining, gill netting, purse-seining, hand lining, and cage trapping.

拖網

拖網分成 ①「單拖」、②「雙拖」、③「蝦拖」及 ④「摻繒」四種模式。

雙拖即有兩艘漁船各拉著拖曳袋型漁網一端，然後同時前進，在包羅推進過程中把在底層棲息的海產一網打盡。長洲以往有不少蝦艇，一般於四十至八十米深的海底進行拖網。漁民將蝦艇用的網罟（亦稱「蝦罟」）從舷外兩旁的叉架垂下，艇開動時便貼近海床拖行，把魚蝦等各類海產捕入漁網內。

Trawling

Trawling can be divided into ① "stern trawling", ② "pair trawling", ③ "shrimp trawling" and ④ "hang trawling".

In pair trawling, two vessels harvest simultaneously, each holding one side of a net. Workers would lower nets close to the seabed; as the boat moves forward, sea creatures are captured easily.

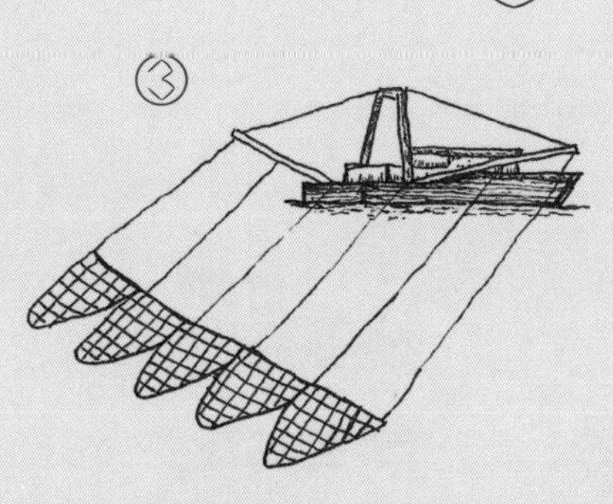

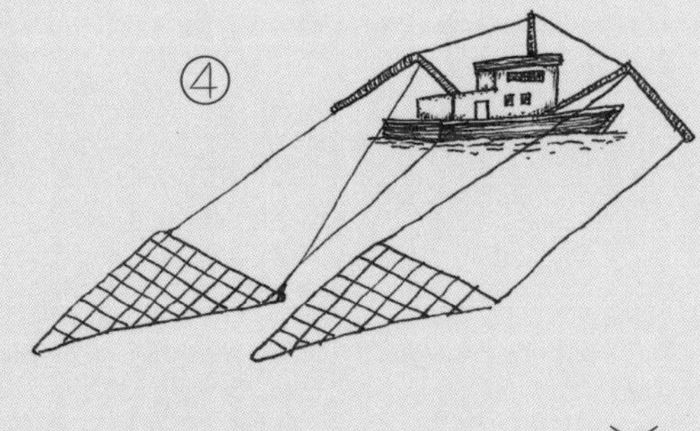

拖網雖是魚產量最高的捕撈方式，但亦對海床造成災難性的破壞。香港政府終於2012年底立法禁止漁民在香港水域進行拖網捕魚，以保護生態環境，並使遭受損害的海洋資源得以盡快復原。

While trawling produces the highest yield, it has a disastrous impact on seabed. In late 2012, the Hong Kong government finally outlawed trawling in local waters. The move was made to conserve native ecology and facilitate restoration of affected marine resources.

延繩釣

傳統捕魚技藝，釣具的主幹是稱爲延繩的長膠絲，掛有多枚魚鈎、短膠絲、浮球和浮標旗。每個釣鈎都裝有魚餌，以誘捕魚類。

Long Lining

A traditional capture technique, long lining involves a long plastic string adorned with multiple baited hooks, short plastic lines, as well as floating balls and markers.

圍網／罟網

大部份圍網漁船都在夜間作業，母船備有大光燈，照射海面以引導魚群結集，當魚達至一定數量後，附設的舢舨就會以圓弧形航行放網圍魚，繼而迅速收緊網底，以防魚群從網下逃走。圍網漁船多用網眼較細小的罟網，因此亦稱「罟仔艇」。

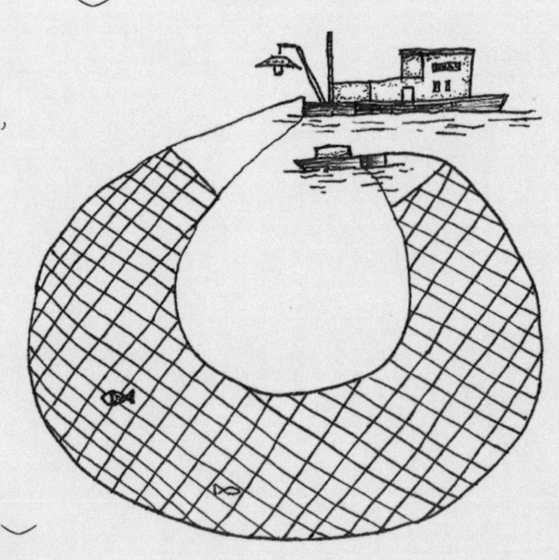

Purse Seining

Most purse seining vessels operate at night. The main vessel is equipped with a strong light that attracts fish. As a sizeable group gathers, neighbouring sampans would lower their nets while moving in an arc, encircling the fish, then quickly close up the bottom. Purse seining is usually done using nets with finer mesh.

刺網

把長方形的刺網放進海中，頂部繫上浮標，底部則加上鉛錘，在海中形成一幅垂直張開的網牆，當魚群撞進網眼內，不能穿越或逃脫而被捕獲。

Gill Netting

A rectangular gillnet is lowered into the sea, with a floating marker on top and a weight at the bottom.

It forms a vertical, moving wall in the water, trapping any fish that encounters it.

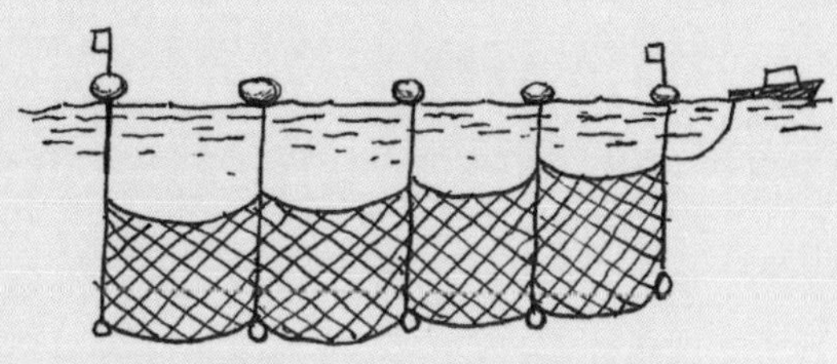

手釣

以魚絲、魚鈎和魚餌垂釣。深海手釣作業的漁民會駕釣艇出海，再分乘舢舨進行手釣。

Hand Lining

Hand lining involves lines, hooks, and bait. Deep sea hand lining workers take to the waters on a larger boat, then fish on separate sampans.

浸籠

屬小型捕魚法，鐵絲魚籠內放置誘魚餌，吸引泥鯭、蝦蟹等海產，而籠的入口又經過特別設計，令獵物易進難逃。

Immersion Cage

A small-scale capture method. Bait is placed in wire cages to attract sea creatures such as crustaceans and mottled spinefoot. Specially designed cage doors facilitate entrance but not exit to minimise escapes.

Jyu Zi Sik Tong 漁子食堂

漁子食堂
兩代漁民的不捨與放下

2019 年 1 月 17 日，阿 Lam 一家把「肥記」賣掉，在筲箕灣看着肥記遠去，老婆群蒂哭成淚人，阿 Lam 雙眼通紅，但強忍着，不流下男兒淚。「肥記」是他們生活了近三十年的漁船，也是他們的生命的一部分。賣掉肥記，代表幾十年漁民生涯正式結束。

阿 Lam，人稱「肥佬」或「肥記」，有十兄弟姊妹，祖籍珠海，早期隨父親揸「大頭艇」，在珠海攞魚到長洲賣，立魚、龍蝦、石斑等生猛海鮮都是他們的「網中物」。那是內地未開放的年代，魚在內地只賣得幾毫一斤，長洲有幾蚊斤，因此他們家的船經常兩邊走。到他這一代，正式落戶長洲。

阿 Lam 小時候的長洲記憶，仍是個人少少的小島，「那時仲未填海，現時的北帝廟球場仍是海。」由於長洲當時仍未有避風塘，一得知打風便要開船到澳門避風。在海上，總有二、三十艘相識的艇泊在一起，阿 Lam 結識了隔離船的張群蒂，無獨有偶，她也有十兄弟姐妹，日久自然生情，順理成章，二人結婚生子，兩公婆打魚維生。

後來，阿 Lam 的兄弟分家，各有各做，他被迫「上街」（指由水上轉為岸上生活），在貨櫃碼頭工作。有人追求陸上的安定，但他更習慣海上的自由，「『上街』好悶，一直以來習慣無王管，去打工卻要被時間綁住。」他記得有一次八號風球，他和同事晚上爬上七個貨櫃頂去綁緊貨櫃，豈料身旁的同事被風吹走，幸好大命不死，但阿 Lam 嚇到翌日便辭職。兜了一圈，最終還是回歸大海，買下一架細船，一年後賺到錢，再轉大船，轉做「鮮艇」（類似於私人批發商，既會出海捕魚，也會收購海產，再散賣給街市內的海鮮零售商），名為「肥記」，一做廿七、八年。

上世紀八十年代尾至九十年代初，由於內地未開放，香港的漁業發展蓬勃，阿 Lam 見到商機，靈機一觸開拓新的生意模式，由捕魚轉型為收魚，即是收內地的漁獲，在香港轉售，一手交一手。阿 Lam 指：「當時生意額起碼十萬一日！海龍蝦一日可以收到十幾擔（約一千斤），二、三十萬一日。」兒子阿豪憶述：

「試過成隻船都係龍蝦！有些死掉賣不出去的龍蝦，夾硬食，食到嘔，發高燒，現在聞到龍蝦陣味都想嘔。」

鮮艇生意看似風光，但其實都是辛苦錢。阿豪說：「我記得父母二人日頭收龍蝦，晚上捉魚，再『車』（開船）回來賣魚，不斷重複，日夜不眠不休地工作。」群蒂指：「嗰時無錢，唔覺得辛苦，又唔驚死，後來諗返先識驚。」

最驚險的經歷，莫過於遇上海盜。那晚阿 Lam 和群蒂如常開船，「車」到石鼓洲尾，妻子負責開船，阿 Lam 稍作休息，忽然一把不知哪來的開山刀，割斷了對講機的線。群蒂憶述：「他（海盜）一枝槍指住阿 Lam 的魂精，一把刀項在我肩上，我好冷靜地跟他說，我們只是做生意的，錢不多，貨就有，你要就拿去吧！」最後那海盜拿了幾千蚊，連麵包都攞埋，只留下阿 Lam 母親留下來的金牌信物。反高潮的是，他離開時跟二人說，他認錯船……最終二人只是破財，是不幸中之大幸，「最緊要人無事，如果他一不小心『搲雞』（開槍），就死㗎咯喎！」阿 Lam 說起來猶有餘悸。

漁民生活驚濤駭浪，去年終於畫上句號。今年，兒子阿豪和妻子阿茵在長洲開設「漁子食堂」，一家人總在店內坐鎮，幫忙打點。餐廳內不忘掛上一張漁船的畫，雖不是「肥記」本尊，但是相同型號。餐廳的餐牌也加入啟發自漁民的食譜，如主打菜式「籠仔飯」，參考漁民的有味飯，即是在船上把蝦乾魚乾等海味放進飯裡一起煲，簡單卻滋味，阿茵說：「希望別人也能嚐到這種味道。」還有酸魷魚米線，鮮魷魚配上酸菜、芽菜、枝竹等配料，酸辣適中，十分開胃。

阿豪和阿茵都是漁民二代，阿茵家人開蝦艇，兩人小時候都有跟父母開船，他們笑言小時候在船上有條「狗尾」，像綁狗一樣把小朋友綁在一起，以免他們跌落海。小學有段時間阿豪到香港仔讀書，但跟父親阿 Lam 一樣，生性愛自由，一放假就回長洲開船。在船上消遣不多，都是打遊戲機，以及聽父母「講耶穌」，他打趣地說：「他倆一個教我分咩魚打咩魚，另一個教我做人道理，講來講去『三幅屁』。」

海上的危險，阿豪亦有深切體會。十一、二歲那年，他跟父母開船，豈料撞到礁石，「望住天花跌落嚟，在海中心叫救命無人應」，那種徬徨無助，至今仍是一道陰影，自此以後很少跟父母開船。當父親阿 Lam 賣「肥記」前問他應否賣船，阿豪二話不說：「即刻賣！」一家人都認為，做漁民高風險，在漁船工作，多體力勞動，尤其是經常彎腰、蹲下，令到父母雙腳經常發痛，甚至彎曲彎形。現在回想起來，阿 Lam 兩夫妻都直指，「如果有得揀，寧願喺岸上洗大餅都好過喺船。做漁民好辛苦。」

口裡說不，但到真正跟「肥記」說再見時，阿豪還是忍不住流下男兒淚，阿豪的兒子柏謙笑說：「呢個人十年都唔喊，嗰日喊到豬頭咁！」後來阿豪輾轉做過地盤，學過廚，到現在開餐廳，縱不在海上，卻不忘本，故名為「漁子」，漁民之子，而在「肥記」上學會的那「三幅屁」，現在仍銘記於心，「人哋點對你，你就點對返人；人哋對你唔好，一次過就算啦，不要斤斤計較，大方啲。」

無論去到哪兒，他們都不會忘記那些大海教會他們的事。

漁子食堂
EXIT 出口
漁子食堂
漁漁子子食食堂堂 長長洲洲香香港港

永佳

永佳

CM63797A
珠万4158
珠万4158

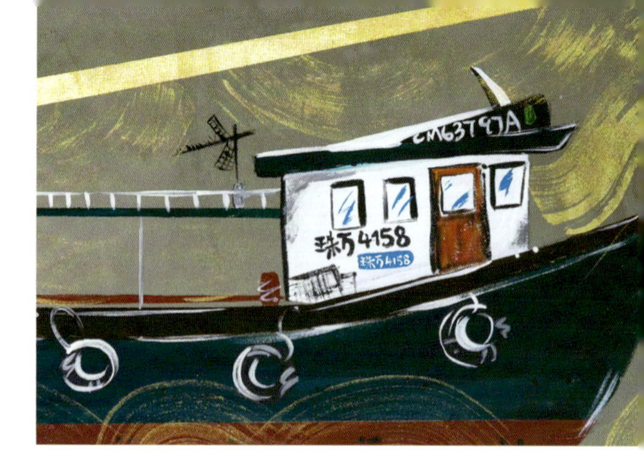

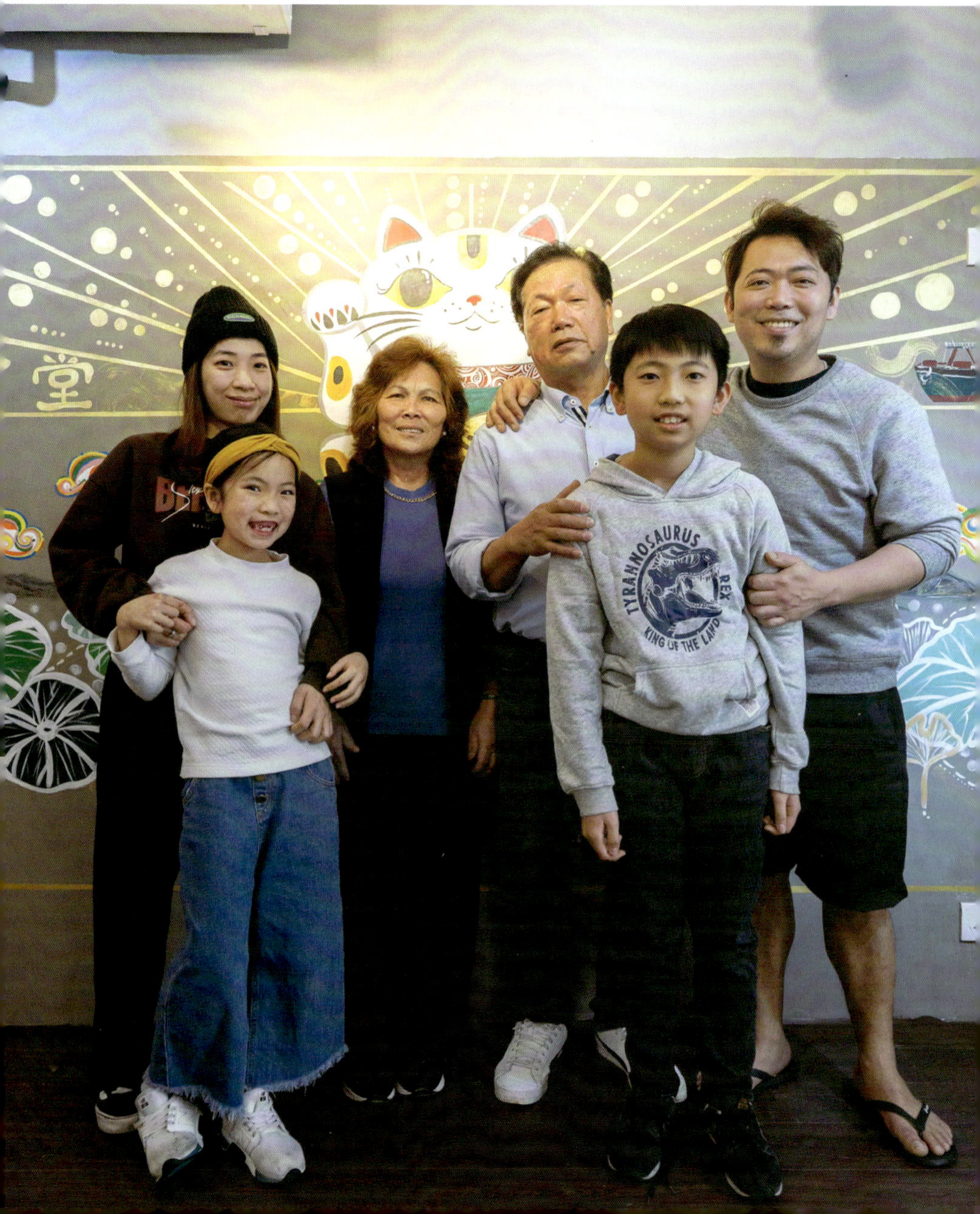
堂
TYRANNOSAURUS REX
KING OF THE LAND

Former Fishermen **ON LETTING GO AND MOVING ON**

On 17 Jan 2019, Lam's family sold *Fat Kee*. As they watched the boat sail off, Lam fought back tears while his wife Kwun Tai started sobbing next to him. Fat Kee was the fishing boat they'd called home for close to three decades; with the boat gone, the couple's lives as fishermen have finally come to an end.

Lam came from a Zhuhai family with ten siblings. In the early years of his career, Lam helped his father fish in Zhuhai, gathering lobsters, groupers and the like to be sold on Cheung Chau. Before the opening up of the Mainland market, fish from those waters could only be sold for less than a dollar per catty, compared to several dollars per catty on Cheung Chau. That's why they often travelled to the island, where Lam eventually settled down.

The Cheung Chau of Lam's childhood was a sparsely populated small island. "That was before reclamation works—the playground today at Pak Tai Temple was still part of the sea." Since a typhoon shelter was yet to be built, everyone had to sail to Macau as soon as they learned the news of approaching storms.

There would always be 20 to 30 boats docking in the waters. Lam met and fell in love with Kwun Tai, who lived on a neighbouring boat and had nine siblings like himself. They got married, had children, and fished for a living.

Lam's siblings eventually went separate ways. He was left with no choice but to move to the city and work at a container terminal. While many are appealed by the stability of urban life, Lam preferred the freedom of living at the sea. "It was so boring," he recalls. "I wasn't used to being managed with a tight schedule." During a No. 8 Typhoon, he and a coworker had to climb on top of seven containers to secure them. His coworker was blown away by the gale and only survived by sheer luck. Terrified, Lam quit his job the next day.

In the end, it had to be the sea. Lam returned to the fishing business, and later operated as a private wholesaler under the name *Fat Kee* for around 28 years.

Hong Kong's fishing industry boomed between late 80s and early 90s. Lam saw a business opportunity—buying yields from the Mainland and selling them in Hong Kong. "We made at least HK$10,000 a day back then! With sea lobsters, we could receive 1000 catties a day, that meant HK$20,000 to HK$30,000."

His son Ho adds, "There were times when the boat was filled with lobsters and we had to eat some of the dead ones. I got sick and developed a high fever once—just the smell nauseates me even today."

Despite impressive profits, the wholesale business was physically exhausting. Ho remembered his parents buying lobsters during the day and fishing at night, then returning to the island to sell their yield. Kwun Tai says, "We were poor, so we didn't feel like the work was too demanding or dangerous. It's only in retrospect that I knew it was too much."

Of all the close calls, the most terrifying was a run-in with a pirate. The couple were heading to Shek Kwu Chau island on a usual work night. When Kwun Tai was on the wheel as Lam was taking a break, a large knife appeared out of nowhere and cut off their walkie-talkie line. "The man pointed a gun at Lam's temple and a knife to my shoulder." Kwun Tai recounts, "I told him calmly, 'We're just running a business and don't have much cash. Take our cargo if you want.'" The pirate took a few thousand dollars and some bread, only leaving a piece of gold jewellery from Lam's mother. As he departed, he told the couple that he'd mistaken theirs for another boat. "We weren't injured, which was the most important part." Lam adds, "If he'd fired by accident, we could've died right there!"

Lam's turbulent life at sea finally came to an end in 2019. In 2020, his son Ho and daughter-in-law Yan launched a diner on Cheung Chau. It features a painting of a fishing boat—not exactly *Fat Kee*, but the same model—and a menu inspired by fishermen's culture. Their signature dish, for example, was a take on the community's beloved 'flavoured rice', a simple staple of rice steamed with a variety of dried seafood. Yan says, "We hope that outsiders can have a taste too." Another popular dish is

the rice noodles served with fresh squid and a perfectly balanced sour and spicy broth.

Ho and Yan are both second-generation fishermen. Yan's family operated a shrimp boat. Both recall tagging along on fishing trips as children, during which the little ones were tied together by a rope to prevent them from falling into the sea. The only distractions onboard were video games or listening to his parents' Christian talk. Ho jokes, "One of them taught me all about fish, while the other taught morals; it was always the same boring spiel over and over." Ho went to school in Hong Kong for some time, but always returned to Cheung Chau during holidays.

Ho also witnessed first-hand the dangers of the sea. At the age of 11 or 12, he was on a regular trip with his parents when they unexpectedly hit a reef. "We watched the ceiling fall, and cried for help to no avail in the middle of the ocean." Such trauma kept Ho from joining most of their subsequent fishing trips. When Lam asked if he should sell the boat, Ho said yes immediately. Both Lam and Kwun Tai state frankly, "If we had the choice, working on land would have been much better. It's a hard life being a fisherman." Repetitive straining motions had left them with aches and even deformations in their feet.

That said, when it came the time to bid *Fat Kee* farewell, Ho couldn't hold back his tears. His son Pak Him says with a laugh, "He could go ten years without crying, but still turned into a sobbing mess that day." After having tried out construction work and culinary training, Ho launched a restaurant rooted in his family's heritage.

The diner's name jyu zi（漁子）literally means "the fisherman's son". The "boring spiel" that he'd learned on Fat Kee remains guiding lights in his heart. "Treat others in the same way they treat you. If someone wronged you, let it go and be generous," Ho says.

Floatudio Cheung Chau

Floatudio 長洲遊艇

Floatudio 長洲遊艇
八十後情侶以海為家

在島上遇見羅家健（Rex）和葉翠霞（Sarah），總是腳踏一對人字拖，穿 T-shirt 短褲或闊腳褲，頭上架一副太陽眼鏡，皮膚曬得黝黑，很難想像七年前，他們仍是在職場打滾的中環白領。

Rex 是長洲人，上兩代都是漁民，自小在長洲長大，畢業後在某英、美資合股公司做 I.T。Sarah 是大埔人，未搬到長洲前，在一家荷蘭公司從事電子商貿經理。2015 年，二人厭倦打工生活，毅然辭職，去環遊世界，走遍三十八個國家，坐順風車、打工換宿，什麼都試過。回港後，他們決定在長洲買下二手遊艇，創立「長洲遊艇」(Floatudio)，在船上過活，靠載客人出海維生。

驟耳聽是夢寐以求的生活，但其實有苦自己知。船上起初無冷氣，無熱水洗澡，冬冷夏熱不在話下，日常打理船隻，事無大小一腳踢，維修、保護、油費等等都是錢，不是想像中輕鬆。頭兩年經營入不敷支，試過銀行戶口剩下三位數。捱了兩年，二人一度想放棄，回歸打工生活，幸好堅持下來，到 2020 年換了新船，生意才上軌道。Sarah 笑言：「如果不是那一年窮遊世界，我不可能由一個穿高踭鞋的港女，變到現在會摺起褲管濕住腳洗廁所。」

Rex 的上兩代都是漁民，爸爸那一代做釣船，遠航至東沙群島，八、九十年代釣東星斑，「車」一轉動輒賺幾十萬。但父親沒有想過要子承父業，「他們認為做漁民無出息，又危險，從小便甚少讓我們踏足漁船。以往他們跨境捕漁，不時被當地軍方開槍掃射，你可以見到長洲很多舊漁船船身都有子彈孔。」父親自從 Rex 的妹妹出世後，就沒有出海捕漁。

自小 Rex 家教甚嚴，不讓他游水，但他卻放學自己偷偷游，游完等到身乾透才敢回家，就連買船，他也是先斬後奏，「我對海的慾望好強。」

直到經歷過風浪，才明白父親常說的危險為何物。有次客人想到索古群島，他們明知有雷暴將至，風力可達八號風球，但客人堅持出航，於是他們照開船，剛過了石鼓洲，一個個比船頭更高的巨浪湧來，嚇得全船人穿好救生衣，作最壞打算，幸好最後相安無事。

每次遇着打風，Rex 和 Sarah 都會留在船上，見船纜唔對路要立即修正。「天鴿」、「山竹」連續兩個大風，整艘船都震，兩人要整晚輪流看守，無得訓。

很多關於船和海上生活的知識，都來自漁民出身的 Rex 的父親，Rex 常說：「要不是有爸爸幫忙，我們的船應該第一年便玩完。」因為這遊艇，他跟仍然熱愛大海的父親有了更多共同話題，父親有空上船整吓嘢，多個地方流連。

除了 junk boat party，Rex 和 Sarah 也積極推廣漁民文化，以及從事海洋保育工作，並於 2019 年成立非牟利機構 Eco Cheung Chau，帶人認識長洲漁業和海洋生態。

兩年前，機緣巧合下，他們得到 WWF 的資助開辦生態團，後來他們與蘇格蘭的大學合作進行海豚探索，在船尾安裝聲納探測器，聽海豚和江豚的行蹤，八個月內一星期一次在大嶼山航行。因這研究工作，Sarah 深刻體會到人類，尤其是大型基建工程如何破壞海洋生態，「有一次我親眼見到一隻海豚媽媽，托住死去很久的海豚 BB 屍體游泳，讓牠可以呼吸。海豚跟我們一樣是哺乳類動物，有感情，那海豚媽媽不願接受自己的孩子已死去，我們全部人都看到哭。」

二人亦與長洲漁民合作，開辦漁民編織漁網工作坊；Sarah 在島上收集和紀錄日漸失傳的「水話」（水上人方言），「這些東西，我哋唔學，有一日就再無人識。」

Floatudio Cheung Chau: **FROM CITY PROFES-SIONALS TO BOAT PARTY HOSTS**

Rex and Sarah now always wear T-shirts, shorts and flip-flops, with sunglasses on top of their heads, but the suntanned couple were white-collar professionals only seven years ago.

Rex, a Cheung Chau native raised by a fishing family, pursued an I.T. career at a foreign corporation upon graduation. Sarah, who hailed from Tai Po, used to work as an e-commerce manager for a Dutch company. In 2015, the couple quit their jobs to travel the world on a shoestring budget, getting a taste of a completely different lifestyle while journeying across 38 countries. After returning to Hong Kong, they purchased a second-hand yacht and shifted to a life at sea, running a junk boat rental business for tourists. This was the beginning of The Floatudio Cheung Chau.

Such a dreamy life posed a myriad of challenges however. There was neither air conditioning nor hot water for the shower on the boat. Rex and Sarah had to take care of maintenance and operation through all kinds of weather, not to mention paying the bills for necessities such as repairs and fuel. The first two years were so tough that the couple almost gave up. They persevered nevertheless and business began to look up after having switched to a new boat in 2020. Sarah says with a laugh, "If it weren't for that year of budget travel, I wouldn't have gone from a city girl in heels to rolling up my pants and cleaning the toilet with wet feet."

Rex comes from generations of fishermen. His father's routes reached as far as the Pratas Islands, often making small fortunes with yields of groupers in the 80s and 90s. However, his father never expected Rex to take over the family business. "People of my father's generation think that fishing is a lowbrow and dangerous job, so they rarely let us on the vessels," Rex says. "They were sometimes shot at by local militants when they fished in other regions—you can still find bullet holes on lots of old fishing vessels on Cheung Chau." After the birth of Rex's younger sister, his father stopped sailing altogether.

Rex's parents forbade him from swimming when he was a child, but he often went secretly after school and headed home only after all his clothes had dried. He didn't even tell his parents about the yacht until after the purchase. Rex says, "I always have a tremendous desire for the sea."

Rex would later come face-to-face with the danger his father had warned him against. A customer once insisted on visiting the Soko Islands despite a thunderstorm warning. They set off reluctantly and came across waves higher than the boat's head, which prompted everyone to put on their life jackets in preparation for the worst. Fortunately, nothing tragic happened in the end.

Whenever there is a typhoon, Rex and Sarah stay on the boat in case they need to fix any issues right away. Throughout these sleepless nights, they often take turns on watch as the entire boat trembles in the storm.

Much of Rex's knowledge of boat maintenance and living at sea comes from his father. Rex says, "Without my dad's help, it would've been game over for us in the first year." This yacht turns out to give the couple more shared topics to talk about, and Rex's father, who is still passionate about the sea, enjoys fixing things around the boat in his spare time.

Apart from hosting junk boat parties, Rex and Sarah are dedicated to conserving fishing culture and marine life. They founded the non-profit Eco Cheung Chau in 2019 to educate the public on the island's fishing industry and ecosystem.

Two years ago, the couple created eco-tours with funding from the WWF. In collaboration with a Scottish university, they installed sonar detectors on their boat to learn about dolphins' travelling habits over eight months. The research showed Sarah how human activities—especially large-scale infrastructure construction work—could devastate the ocean. "Once I saw a mother dolphin holding up the long-dead body of her baby so that it could breathe," Sarah says. "Dolphins are mammals with emotions just like us. That mother couldn't accept her baby's death. We all cried watching her."

Rex and Sarah also partner with Cheung Chau fishermen to host workshops on net weaving in the hope to pass on the craft. Meanwhile, Sarah has been documenting the Water Dialect (shui wa, 水話), the fast-disappearing language of fishing communities, driven by the mission to conserve important cultural artifacts of the island before they become lost in time.

① **大撈面／細撈面** daai6 lou1 min6 / sai3 lou1 min6

意思：左邊／右邊。

「撈面」是那邊的意思，船頭以左為「大撈面」，船頭以右則是「細撈面」。

② **打石湖** daa2 sek6 wu4

意思：打雷。

有說法指漁民在船頭放掃帚或男孩瀨過尿的床墊，可以避過「打石湖」。

③ **車大叻** ce1 daai6 lek6

意思：開船。漁民會叫開船做「車」船。

④ **白確** baak6 kok3/ kot3

意思：發泡膠箱。每次出海漁民都需要準備大量發泡膠箱放冰，以保存漁獲。

⑤ **落舌** lok6 sit3

意思：加冰。

如上所述，漁民需要大量冰去保存漁獲。雪跟「舌」發音相近，意指冰。

⑥ **乾屍** gon1 si1

意思：薑絲。

⑦ **大雞札** daai6 gai1 zaat3

意思：大甲由

⑧ **姑肉** gu1 juk6

意思：舊毛巾或舊漁網肉，清潔洗刷用。

鳴謝：船到橋頭生活節、浪長洲

Shui Wa

The Disappearing Dialect of Fishing Communities

Why is the name Hong Kong spelled as it is, instead of 'Heung Kong', which is closer to its Cantonese pronunciation? Some say that early British colonists hired fishermen as guides, who called the area "Hong Kong" in their dialect.

Fishing communities have a long history in the city, accompanied by its unique culture and language. Their dialect is also known as Tanka or Shui Wa. As fishing communities became marginalised due to social development, many families faced discrimination over their accent and parents stopped teaching the language at home. The use of Shui Wa has therefore been in steady decline.

In 2017, an arts festival hosted by Cheung Chau Wave prompted Sarah Yip, co-director of The Floatudio Cheung Chau, to document and collect data on the dialect. Sarah then collaborated with speech therapist Tiff Chan to develop a Shui Wa learning system. While some of its vocabularies might sound like twisted versions of Cantonese, Shui Wa features remarkably unique phrases that describe working on the sea and showcase the daily wisdom of fishing communities.

水話

逐漸失傳的水上人方言

大家可有想過，為什麼香港的英文，是 Hong Kong，而不是更為接近其發音的 Heung Kong？有說，當年英軍登陸香港，由蜑家婦人阿群帶路，水上人叫香港做「康港」，因此英文名譯做 Hong 而非 Heung。水上人在香港生活多年，有其獨特的文化和語言，水上人話，又稱為蜑家話或「水話」。隨着社會發展，水上人身份被邊緣化，不少漁民及子女都因其口音而被岸上人歧視，久而久之，父母都不再教小朋友講「水話」，令這方言逐漸失傳。

2017年，藝術組織「浪長洲」的藝術節，促使長洲遊艇的主理人之一 Sarah 開始在島上向漁民收集和記錄水話，跟言語治療師陳曉蕾（Tiff）合作，發展出一套學習水話的系統。有些詞彙聽上去像是讀歪了音的廣東話，但當中不少詞彙跟海上工作息息相關，蘊藏水上人的生活智慧。

① **大撈面 / 細撈面** *daai6 lou1 min6 / sai3 lou1 min6*

Left / Right. *Lou1 min6* means 'that side'; left of the bow is *daai6 lou1 min6* (big side), while right of the bow is *sai3 lou1 min6* (small side).

② **打石湖** *daa2 sek6 wu4*

Thunder. Some believe that placing a broom or mattress wetted by a boy at the vessel's bow provides protection from thunder.

③ **車大叻** *ce1 daai6 lek6*

Driving a boat. The character for 'vehicle' is used here.

④ **白確** *baak6 kok3/ kot3*

Styrofoam boxes. In preparation for each trip, fishermen must prepare large quantities of styrofoam boxes packed with ice to preserve their catch.

⑤ **落舌** *lok6 sit3*

To add ice. The character for 'tongue' is used here because its similar pronunciation to 'snow'.

⑥ **乾屍** *gon1 si1*

Julienned ginger. The similar sounding characters literally say 'dried corpse'.

⑦ **大雞札** *daai6 gai1 zaat3*

Large cockroach. The similar sounding characters literally say 'large chicken wrap'.

⑧ **姑肉** *gu1 juk6*

Old towels or fishing nets for cleaning and scrubbing.

Special thanks to the Inter-island Festival and Cheung Chau Wave.

西灣村民阿翠

A Sai Wan Villager

本村擴建落成
政務司
鍾逸傑司憲蒞臨揭幕
爰勒貞珉以垂永紀
WAS OPENED BY
SECRETARY FOR DISTRICT ADMINISTRATION
ON

西灣村民阿翠
推廣傳統漁民文化

停泊在岸邊大大小小的漁船和艇仔，既是長洲獨有的風景，也是長洲漁業曾經興盛的憑證。以往水上人起居生活都在船上，直到六十年代，漁民陸續「上街」，搬到岸上生活，而長洲最早期的漁民村落，是位於離渡輪碼頭廿分鐘腳程的西灣美經援村。

阿翠在西灣長大，家族幾代都是漁民，村內的事，她瞭如掌。我們跟她到西灣走一圈，首先遇見村口一棵高大的細葉榕，樹下人們供奉土地公公保佑村民出入平安。樹旁的碑帖寫上村子的由來：1966 年，長洲鄉事委員主席周理炳、馮北財和地方鄉者姚啟亨向美經援會（美國經濟援助協會，Care U.S.A）申請資助建村，由姚啟亨先生廉價讓出耕地建村，西灣美經援村和應善良美經援村分別於 1968 和 1969 年落成，至於第三期自助美經援村，則於 1972 年落成。

我們先由榕樹沿斜路往上走，一直到西園的入口處，左轉，即見到一排兩層高的房子，屋外不約而同都有一片小空地，作為室內空間的伸延，讓途人一窺屋主的生活。我們在路口轉進錯綜複雜的村子，在屋外的長走廊上來回穿梭，要不是有村民帶路，應早已迷路。不難發現，廚房通常設於室外，而村子的樓梯扶手和室外走廊的欄杆都塗上亮眼的紅色，是為村子添個性？除了房屋，村內也有公廁，阿翠指，第一期的村子沒有抽水馬桶，因此村內曾經有四座公廁和浴室，亦有過鄉村福利中心、幼稚園等公共設施。阿翠又指，村內從前有紙牌廠、電子廠、潛水衣廠，更有個「海膽佬」，把捉回來的海膽包裝好，一板一板船運到日本，是個小而完備的聚落。

村子的房屋最初只有一層，後來擴建至兩層高，建於山坡上的房子，有不少居民自製的設備。阿翠邊走邊指出隨處可見的「漁民智慧」：村民自行搭建的支柱和簷蓬、架在鐵柱之上用來曬魚乾蝦乾的漁網、由雪櫃變身而成的儲物空間、村民自建的用來乘涼和打「遊糊」（東莞牌）的亭子等等，沒有現代高樓大度的井井有條，卻富有庶民的生命力和創意。

與阿翠見面時，時值西灣大節天后誕。阿翠一大早就在西灣的天后廟打點大小事務，或許是天雨關係，到廟參拜的人不多。她記得兒時的天后廟熱鬧得很，現時快樂之友士多後面是戲棚，有戲看的日子，漁船泊滿整個西堤，像戲院座位一樣，一排一排，等着睇大戲。

阿翠自小在船上生活，直到讀書的年紀便住在西灣親戚家，每逢假期則回到船上幫手，她笑言在船上長時間住在矮凳，「坐到個『躉』大晒」，同時也練成響亮的嗓門，和一身爽朗。她的祖父母做罟仔，到了父母一代轉做蝦艇，漁穫多的時候，小小艇子變「潛艇」，有一次船都快要沈到水裡去，一船人穿好水泡，作最壞打算，幸好有大船經過，即揮動水上人帽叫救命，最後相安無事。

熱心村內事務的她，2010 年應香港明愛西灣社區發展計劃，連同數十位有漁民背景的街坊籌辦公眾活動，推廣漁民文化，並成立「長洲西灣文化村」，成為文化村的骨幹成員。她總是說：「漁民文化好多故仔！香港也是漁業起家，漁民有很多技術和故事，只因沒有文字記載而失傳。」

出入平安

天后宮

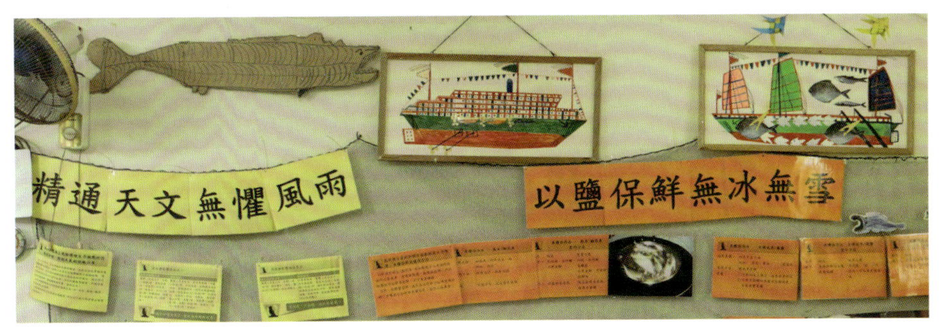
精通天文無懼風雨
以鹽保鮮無冰無雪

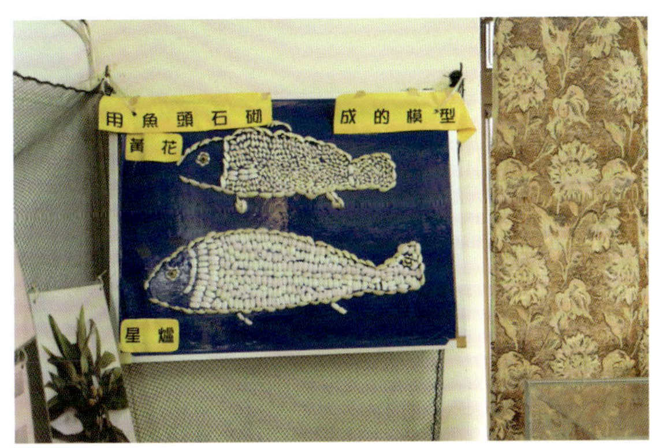
用"魚頭石砌
成的模"型
黃花
星爐

A Sai Wan Villager
PRESERVING FISHING HERITAGE

Fishing vessels and boats of various sizes not only form an essential part of Cheung Chau's landscape, they also mark the bygone heights of the fishing industry. Fishing communities, which have worked and lived on the waters for decades, only moved onshore from the 1960s onwards. Sai Wan CARE Village is the island's earliest fishing village.

From a family of generations of fishermen, Chui grew up in Sai Wan and knew the village inside out. Beneath the tall banyan tree at the entrance are offerings for Tudigong (the deity of the land) to keep villagers in prayer for safe travels. A stone inscription by the tree explains the village's origins: In 1966, Cheung Chau Rural Committee chairpersons Chow Leibing and Fung Bukchoi applied for funding from Care U.S.A. to build the village at a bargain price on the farmland provided by local landowner Yao Kaiheng. The Sai Wan and Ying Sin Leung CARE Villages were completed in 1968 and 1969 respectively. The project's third phase — Self Help CARE Village — was completed in 1972.

On the left of the slope to Saiyuen's entrance is a row of two-storey houses. Each house features a small front yard extended from indoor space, which offers a sneak peek into residents' daily lives. Kitchens are usually set up outdoors. Stairway handrails and corridor barriers are all painted in bright red, and public bathrooms can also be found in the area. The first phase was reportedly built without flush toilets, so it came with four public bathrooms along with communal facilities such as shower rooms, a welfare centre, and a kindergarten. The village also used to house many factories for the manufacturing of cards, electronics, and diving suits, as well as for an 'Urchin Man' who packaged freshly caught sea urchins and shipped them to Japan.

The village was expanded into its current two-storey form after some time. Numerous homemade tools and structures of fishermen's wisdom still adorn the houses on the slope: handcrafted supporting beams and canopies; fishing

nets sitting on metal poles for sun-drying fish and shrimp; refrigerators turned storage compartments; pavilions for chilling out and playing mahjong... such quirks mark the villagers' vivid creativity that is not likely to be found in urban areas.

On the birthday of sea goddess Tin Hau—a major festival for Sai Wan, Chui begins the day early for various tasks at the Sai Wan Tin Hau Temple, though only a few worshippers show up probably due to the rain. Back when Chui was a child, the temple was bustling with activities. The temporary bamboo theatre always attracted a huge crowd on performance days, on which the entire bay area would be lined with rows and rows of fishing boats.

Having grown up on a boat, Chui moved to a relative's place in Sai Wan when she reached school age, and would return to the boat to help out during holidays. "All the sitting left me with a huge bottom," she jokes. Her invigorating voice and cheery demeanor are characteristic of fishing families.

Chui's grandparents engaged in seine fishing, before her parents switched to shrimp trawling. When yields were heavy, their small boat would teeter on the brink of danger. One time the whole crew had to put on lifebuoys to prepare for the worst. Fortunately, a large vessel passing by saw them waving their hats for help and came to their rescue.

Chui remains devoted to the village community. As part of the Caritas Cheung Chau Sai Wan Community Development Project in 2010, she organised public events promoting fishing village culture with dozens of neighbours. She also founded the Cheung Chau Sai Wan Cultural Village, which she still leads. "There are so many stories in fishermen's culture!" Chui notes, "Even Hong Kong first thrived on its fishery. Fishermen have lots of skills and stories, yet these tend to be forgotten due to a lack of written documentation."

春到花含笑
百鳥樹上叫
雲霧罩孝山
春景
春有百花秋有月
夏有涼風冬有雪
若無閒事掛心頭
便是人間好時節
明愛長洲西灣社區發展計

漁民食譜

FISHERMAN'S RECIPES

所謂靠山吃山，靠海吃海，以海爲家的漁民，因生活和工作的實際需要，而衍生出獨特的水上人飲食文化，譬如漁民出海經常一去就是幾日幾夜，船上沒有雪櫃，因此想到用鹽去保持漁獲新鮮。經鹽醃過的魚再經蒸製，肉質嫩滑，淡淡咸味提升魚鮮味，別有一番風味。除了海鮮，他們亦食用多種不同海草，聽說由於漁民經常抵受日曬，體質容易燥熱，故食用寒涼的海草，有些罕有的海草更有祛濕、降燒等功能。以下幾份來自長洲西灣漁民及網上收集而來的傳統食譜，煮出意想不到的美味。

What we eat tells a story of where and how we live. Based on their particular lifestyle, fishing communities have developed a unique food culture rooted in practicality. For example, on fishing trips that often lasted several days, salt was a popular solution to preserve food without refrigeration. The slightly salted fish has a delicate, smooth texture that compliments its natural flavours. Apart from seafood, seaweed is widely consumed by fishing workers. From a Chinese medical perspective, fishermen who are almost always exposed to sunlight should cool their bodies by eating seaweed. Some rare species are even known for lowering temperature and preventing overhydration. Here are several classic recipes from Sai Wan fishermen and online sources all born out of generations of lifetimes at sea.

01

大苔薏米粉腸糖水

SWEET SEAWEED SOUP WITH BARLEY AND PIG CHITTERLINGS

豬粉腸一斤至斤半
Pig Chitterlings
1 to 1.5 catties

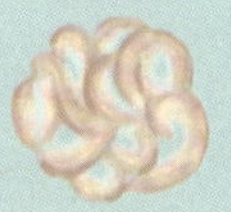

瓜條 (糖冬瓜) 一包
Sugared winter melon
1 packet

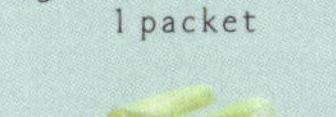

桔餅 (糖柑桔) 三、四隻
Sugared citrus
3 to 4 pieces

大苔 (海草的一種) 四兩
Dai Toi (a type of seaweed)
4 catties

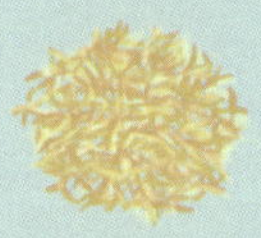

冰糖一包
Rock candy
1 packet

生熟薏米各四兩
Raw and cooked barley
4 taels each

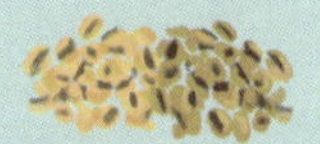

1. 大苔過水泡軟，其他材料洗淨，把所有材料和水放到煲中，
2. 煲至薏米淋身即可，約個半小時。
(提供食譜的阿翠指，通常漁民工作忙碌，通常把材料放進煲內「一鑊熟」，等到工作完結便開餐，因此食譜沒有複雜的步驟。)

1. Rinse and soak seaweed until soft.
2. Wash other ingredients and boil in water for about 1.5 hours, until barley softens.
(According to Ah Chui, who provided the recipe, fishermen usually favour a one-pot approach to save time, and would eat after finishing work. This means that recipes tend not to feature complicated steps.)

鮑魚綠豆沙

ABALONE MUNG BEAN SOUP

鮑魚一斤 Abalone 1 catty 	綠豆 50 克 Mung beans 50g 	黃豆 30 克 Soy beans 30g 	眉豆 30 克 Black-eyed peas 30g 
西尾董 40 克 Sai mei dung 40g 	陳皮 1 塊 Chenpi (sun-dried mandarin orange peel) 1 piece 	生薏米 20 克 熟薏米 10 克 Raw barley 20g Cooked barely 10g 	片糖 1 條 Brown slab sugar 1 piece 

1. 生薏米、綠豆浸過夜。
2. 西尾董浸發至軟身，約三十分鐘。鮑魚起肉洗淨，汆水待用。
3. 水滾後，加入黃豆、眉豆、西尾董、陳皮、生熟薏米，煲約 1.5 小時。
4. 加入綠豆煲至開花。
5. 下片糖調味，最後下鮑魚細火煲約半小時，完成。

1. Soak raw barey and mung beans overnight.
2. Soak sai mei dung for about 30 minutes until soft. De-shell abalone, wash and blanch.
3. Put soy beans, black-eyed peas, sai mei dung, chenpi, raw and cooked barley in boiling water. Boil for approximately 1.5 hours.
4. Add mung beans and cook until soft.
5. Add brown slab sugar to taste. Finally, add abalone and simmer on low heat for about 30 minutes.

咸鮮魚

SALTED FRESH FISH

03

咸鮮食法：原條蒸，或連用蝦和薑粒一起放在飯面蒸，漁民稱之爲「有味飯」。

Salted fresh fish can be steamed whole, or on top of rice with shrimp and chopped ginger. The latter is called 'Flavoured Rice'.

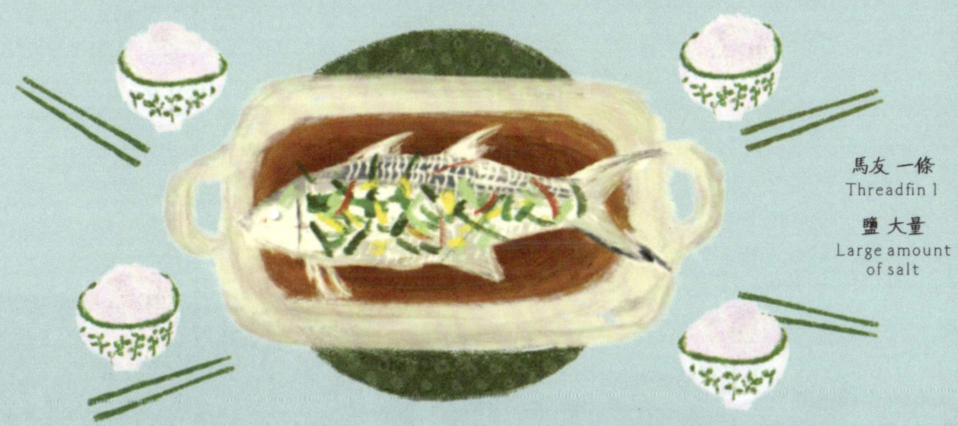

馬友 一條
Threadfin 1

鹽 大量
Large amount of salt

做法一：生拆（不劏肚，原條魚醃製，稱之為生拆。）

Method 1: Salted whole

1. 從魚腮位置挖出魚腸和及內臟，魚身無須打鱗，否則會過咸。
2. 把鹽塞進魚內，放在鋪滿鹽的盆子上，再用鹽覆蓋魚身，醃一晚。
3. 醃好後，把魚浸水十五分鐘到一小時，打魚鱗，曬幾小時即可食用。

（曬咸魚以秋高氣爽，濕度 40-50% 最佳，如太陽過猛會把魚肉曬熟。）

1. Remove intestines and guts from gill opening. Keep scales on to prevent over-salting.
2. Stuff the inside of the fish with salt. Then place the fish in a basin full of salt and make sure it is fully covered. Leave overnight.
3. After salting is complete, soak fish in water for 15 to 60 minutes, then remove scales. The fish will be ready to serve after drying for a few hours in the sun. (Salted fish is best dried on autumn days with a humidity of 40–50% . The fish wound be overcooked if the sun is too strong.)

做法二：披開（先把魚劏開到醃製的，稱為披開或披花帶）

Method 2: Cut open before salting

1. 先打魚鱗，從背部把魚劏開，起骨，斬掉魚頭，去腸。
2. 在盆子上鋪上廚房紙，放上魚，再灑上薄薄一層鹽，曬兩、三小時即可食用。

1. Remove scales. Cut the fish open from the back, remove bones, head, and intestines.
2. Place fish on a basin lined with kitchen towel. Lightly sprinkle a thin layer of salt. The fish will be ready to serve after drying for two to three hours in the sun.

末代修船匠牛哥

Bull the Last Ship Repairer

末代修船匠牛哥
半生守住失傳技藝

七十年代香港漁業發展蓬勃，連帶補船行業興起。人稱牛哥的黃志賢憶述：「舊時單單長洲就有八、九間船廠，專門裝船，排廠就有三、四間，負責維修。數百隻船泊滿整個木灣，場面非常墟冚。每逢冬天少雨水天氣爽，生意更旺。」廠與廠之間競爭激烈，全盛時期數十位師傅沸沸騰騰地一同開工。「那時嚴重缺人，只要你識揸鎚仔就會推你入行。」牛哥十一歲就到父親經營的船排廠學師，現在是錦興船排廠的東主，一做就是半生。

當年雖然工作不斷，但修船匠卻毫無保障。「往時薪酬以日計，早上八時開工，但要是十時下雨要停手的話，也就賠了那兩小時的人工，最多得餐飯食，好淒涼。要快到八十年代工會成立後，才爭取到按鐘計。」牛哥找出他的工會會員證，巴掌大的本子，印著蠅頭小楷的會規，翻到最後一頁就是會員的照片和個人資料。牛哥入會時二十五歲，結婚後轉到香港仔造船謀生，直至父親找他幫手才回歸長洲，十七年前正式接手排廠。

「八十年代尾很多船家都改去澳門修船，長洲就一下子冷清下來，好多行家生意不繼就索性關門大吉把地方賣出去，久而久之就愈來愈少人從事這一行。」牛哥語帶唏噓：「不過沒多久澳門又被大陸的取代。以前我們這邊需求高，會直接從暹羅入口木材，樹幹如半個人高，如火水罐那麼粗，然後運到香港仔剘，但近年木材都是先運去大陸，我們再跟他們取貨。」修船屬木工，故工匠們奉魯班為師。「往時每年六月師傅誕，都會在北帝廟船廠附近擺十圍八圍慶祝，有飯派，成班師傅又會一齊坐在岸邊飲燒酒。」

牛哥的排廠現在除了修葺大頭艇和圍網作業的罟仔艇，亦是大型漁船的救星。「超過二十米的漁船其他廠不會做他們生意，就只得找我們幫忙。」客人來自港九新界，訪問當日排上的三艘船，就分別來自屯門、長洲、油麻地。排廠僱了四五位修船匠，當中有兩位正在拿著小油轆為一首木船攢灰。「木船唔襟，要逐處攢灰補油，幾年就要整一次，所以愈來愈多人改用纖維船。纖維鋪上四至五層就不怕河蟲蛀，可以十年先要修葺一次。」每艘船用纜索攪上排後，就可以進行剷蠔殼、重新加釘、攢灰、髹防洪漆等工序。「不過有些問題還是要潛落水底望，所以師傅都要識水性。」牛哥的伙記跟了他十多年，以兄弟相稱。

幽默風趣的牛哥解說生動活潑，坦言沒有修不到的船，對手藝有孜孜不倦的熱忱，只有九年前一次意外才令他閃過退下火線的念頭。他邊笑著憶述，邊把手虛放在攬排用的絞輪上，模仿當時的情況。「那時一個分神，手就跟著絞輪上的單車鏈『彈』（被拖行）了一個圈。幸好條鏈用得耐有點鬆，不然五隻手指早就齊戢戢切斷了。」意外令牛哥左掌尾指爆骨，其餘四指斷根，要動手術駁回。「住了兩天醫院好悶，一出院就回來主持大局，手動不了就拿著大聲公叫班兄弟做。」受傷後除了手指不能完全伸直，其餘動作依然靈活，無礙手藝。

早屆退休年齡的牛哥本打算今年內退下來，但始終捨不得，反正閒著也是飲啤酒、賭馬仔，倒不如繼續開工。「很多熟客都叫我千萬不要退休，不是我自誇，而是真的沒有人做。青衣鐵排只做躉船，筲箕灣就專做遊艇生意，漁船就大抵只有長洲這兩間廠會修。」加上疫情不能北上，漁民就更依賴碩果僅存的本地排廠。

三女之父的他無奈找不到人繼承衣缽，言語間不時透著惋惜。「其實新人跟一兩年就會上手，人工又唔算差，但就算我肯教，都沒有人肯入行啦。」面對這個僅存的工業的沒落、甚至在香港絕跡，他笑說：「所以話，我呢隻老牛是受保護動物啊！」

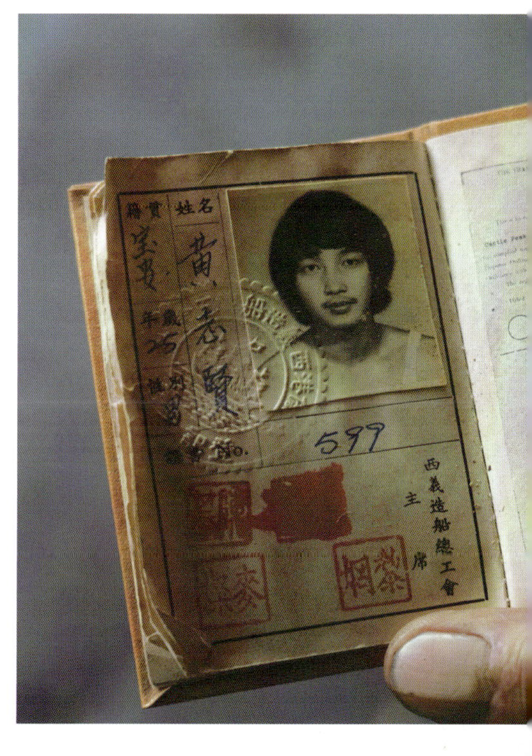
籍貫
姓名
黃志賢
年歲
25
性別
男
No.
599

Brother Bull AND HONG KONG'S LAST SHIP REPAIRERS

Hong Kong's booming fishing industry in the 70s saw the rise of ship-repairing businesses. "In the old days, there were eight to nine shipbuilding factories on Cheung Chau and three to four shipyards that offered repairs," Wong Chi Yin, known on the island as Brother Bull, recalls. "Hundreds of vessels were parked at the main bay. Our business got even busier during the dry winter months." Competition was fierce, and as many as dozens of craftsmen worked at the same time. "We were short on staff; anyone who could use a hammer was ushered in." Bull became an apprentice at his father's shipyard when he was 11 years old. Now the owner of Kam Hing Shipyard, he has dedicated a lifetime to his craft.

Despite hectic work, ship repairers had no employment protection. "Back then we were paid by the day. Work started at 8 a.m. but if we had to stop at 10 a.m. due to rain, those two hours would go unpaid and we would at most get a meal—it was miserable," says Bull. "After a union was formed in the 80s, we finally received hourly pay."

Bull's union ID was a palm-sized booklet with regulations printed in tiny type, and the member's photo and personal details on the last page. Bull was 25 when he joined the union. After getting married, he worked as a shipbuilder in Aberdeen until his father asked him to go home and help out. He officially took over the shipyard 17 years ago.

"At the end of the 80s, customers flocked to get repairs in Macau instead, so businesses on Cheung Chau dwindled. A lot of shipyards closed and sold their land; eventually, most people left this industry." Bull explains. "Business in Macau was then quickly taken over by Mainland China." Back when there was a high demand in Hong Kong, timber was imported from Thailand directly and sent to Aberdeen for processing. But that was no longer the case when the Chinese market gained traction and giant logs were shipped first to the Mainland.

Ship repairing is woodwork, which is why craftsmen in the business worship Lo Pan, the patron saint of Chinese builders and carpenters. "In the old days, on Lo Pan's Birthday in June, we all celebrated with a huge feast near the Pak Tai Temple where most ship factories were. There was free food and all the craftsmen would share a drink at the beach."

Nowadays, Bull's shipyard is not only an important service provider for boats and sampans, but also the sole repairer for large fishing vessels. "Other places don't take vessels over 20 metres. We're the only shipyard that can help." Bull's customers come from everywhere. On the day of the interview, boats at the drydock are from Tuen Mun, Cheung Chau, and Yau Ma Tei. Two of the shipyard's five repairers are plastering a wooden boat. "Wooden vessels deteriorate easily. They require plastering and repainting every few years." That explains why more and more fishermen are switching over to fiberglass boats. "A vessel with four to five layers of fibreglass is resistant to water pest damage, and only requires repair work every ten years."

After hauling the vessel by cables onto the dock, repairers would begin various procedures such as removing barnacles from the boat's bottom, replacing nails and varnishing. "Still, there are certain issues that call for diving under the surface to get a closer look, so all craftsmen have to be skilled swimmers." Bull's employees have been working with him for over a decade, and they refer to each other as brothers.

"There is no vessel I cannot repair," he says. Always passionate about the craft, he had only thought about quitting once, nine years ago after an alarming accident. He laughs while demonstrating what happened at the time: "It was just a moment's lapse in attention. My hand got dragged a full circle by the bike chain on this wheel. Luckily the chain was slightly loose, otherwise all five of my fingers would have been chopped off clean." The accident left Bull with a broken bone in his left pinky finger, and four severed digits that had to be surgically reattached. "I was so bored after a couple of days in the hospital. Once I got discharged, I came back to run the place, giving instructions to my brothers via loudspeaker." Apart from mild impairments in flexibility, his injured hand has recovered perfectly and he can still exercise his craft without any issue to date.

Bull originally intended to retire within this year, but found himself preferring work over idle time spent on drinking beer and betting on horse races. "Many regulars ask me not to retire. I am really not boasting, just that there's no one left to do this job," says the one-of-a-kind veteran. "Shipyards in Tsing Yi only take care of junks, while Sau Kei Wan specialises only in yachts. The only two places that can repair fishing boats are both on Cheung Chau." Since they cannot travel to the Mainland during the pandemic, fishermen have no choice but to rely on local shipyards.

None of Bull's three daughters plans to inherit his business, and he has struggled to find a successor in this dying industry. "It only takes a couple of years to learn the trade, and the pay isn't bad. But even if I'm willing to teach, no one is eager to learn." He sighs and mocks himself with a laugh: "This old bull is an endangered species."

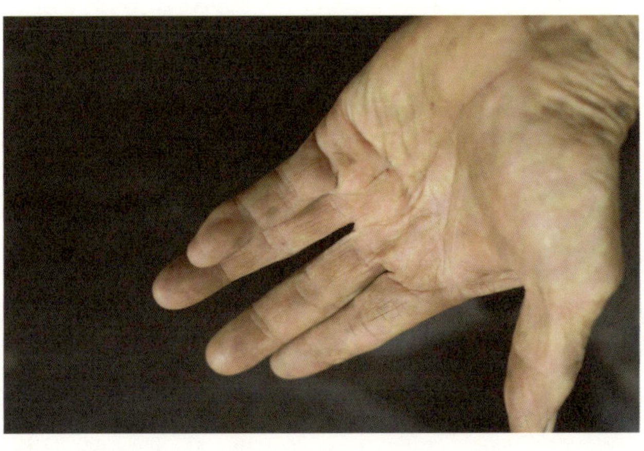

長洲歷史趣聞
FUN HISTORICAL FACTS ABOUT CHEUNG CHAU

青銅時代
BRONZE AGE

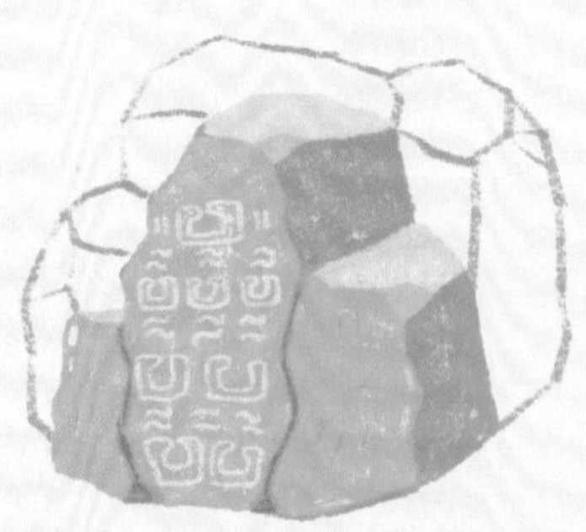

古代石刻
ANCIENT STONE CARVINGS

「東灣古代石刻」位於長洲東南部的黑排路、華威酒店的山坡下，是香港八大古石刻之一，於 1970 被地質學家發現，1982 年列為法定古蹟。雖迄今尚未能確切印證其刻鑿年份，但石刻上有數條環繞著曲線小凹槽構成的紋理，與青銅器時代器物上的紋飾類似，因此可推斷石刻的刻鑿年代大約與青銅器時代同期，即約有三千年歷史之久！

The Tung Wan Ancient Stone Carvings is located on Hak Pai Road, right beneath the slope of Warwick Hotel in the southeast. Considered as one of the eight ancient stone carvings in Hong Kong upon the discovery by geologists in 1970, it has been listed as a Declared Monument since 1982.

Nobody is sure of the exact date and year of its creation, but the motifs formed by the swirly lines and depressions carved into the rocks are similar to the decorative motifs found on objects from the Bronze Age. One can thus deduce that the rock carvings were made during the Bronze Age, a good 3,000 years ago!

1800 – 1910S

張保仔外，與長洲略有淵源的海盜
CHEUNG PO TSAI AND OTHER CHEUNG CHAU PIRATES

香港開埠之初至二次大戰期間，海盜橫行。最為香港人熟悉的，定必是活躍於清朝的傳奇海盜張保仔。張氏坐擁六百艘戰船以及逾四萬名海盜，稱霸廣東沿岸。由於他的船隊主要劫掠官船和外國貨船，從不滋擾貧民和漁戶，又嚴禁屬下姦淫婦女，故被視為劫富濟貧的俠盜。傳說現在旅遊熱點「張保仔洞」，曾是他藏身、藏寶的巢穴之一。

不過，垂涎長洲的海盜又豈止張保仔。1912 年 8 月中，即第十五任港督梅含理抵港履新後一個月，一班為數五十多名海盜夜半登上長洲，先攻陷長洲警署，掠奪警署的槍械彈藥及夾萬內的現金，先後殺死了三名印裔警員，再肆意洗劫了大街上的當舖和商店。

由於當時長洲沒有連接香港的電話或電報，全賴漁民偷偷駕小艇到港島報案，警察總部才得悉此事。但翌日早上派員到場時，海盜早已逃之夭夭……一年後，四名涉案海盜頭目在澳門落網，被引渡回港受審，全遭判處死刑。同年，港英政府為加強防禦，斥資把警署搬到居高臨下的小山丘，亦即在警署徑的現址。

In the period between the early founding days of Hong Kong and the Second World War, pirates had been very active in the region. The most well-known pirate is none other than the legendary Cheung Po Tsai from the Qing Dynasty. Owning more than 600 warships and a crew of 40,000 pirates, Cheung ruled the coasts of Guangdong. His crew only robbed from government fleets and foreign cargo ships. They would not take anything from the fishermen or the poor, and his men were strictly prohibited from mistreating women. That's why he is often viewed as a heroic outlaw. The popular tourist spot Cheung Po Tsai Cave is said to be one of his many hiding spots for his treasures.

Cheung Po Tsai was not the only pirate who preyed on the port of Cheung Chau. In August 1912, one month after Sir Francis Henry May was appointed Governor of Hong Kong, 50 pirates landed Cheung Chau in the middle of the night. The group attacked and captured the Cheung Chau police station, seizing artillery weapons and cash stored in the safe. Three Indian police officers were killed in the incident. Loaded with weapons, the pirates then proceeded to rob all shops on the main streets of Cheung Chau.

There was no landline or telegraph line that connected Cheung Chau with other places in Hong Kong back then. A group of fishermen discreetly sailed to Hong Kong Island to alert the police. However, all the pirates had already fled when officers finally reached Cheung Chau the next morning...

One year later, four key leaders of that pirate group were arrested in Macau. They were extradited to Hong Kong for their trials and sentenced to death. In the same year, to strengthen their defense, the colonial government moved the Cheung Chau police station to the hilltop and that place became its permanent location since.

1940s

消失的殖民地界石
THE MISSING BOUNDARY STONES

眾所周知，英治政府於二十世紀初，將太平山劃為外籍家庭和使節的專用住宅區，但原來長洲的山頂亦曾經歷相同命運！一次大戰後，政府看中了長洲南部的山頂區。即使兩位華人議員極力反對，仍無法阻止立法會於 1919 年通過《長洲（居所）條例》(The Cheung Chau (Residence) Ordinance，1919)，把長洲南部撥作外國教會靈修和外籍人士居住度假之用，嚴禁華人棲身。政府更為此豎立了十五座界碑，沿著西南面的鯆魚灣，延伸至東北端的南蛇塘，以及東灣長洲醫院，把小島的南與北分割。界石約半米高，以花崗岩雕琢而成，呈尖頂方柱狀，刻有法案的縮寫和編號。這項不平等條例直至 1946 年才廢除，較港島的山頂遲了足足十六年始得解放。這些界石雖早已失效，但承載了上百年歷史，只可惜部分已不知所終。

As many people may know, in the early 20th century, the colonial government marked Victoria Peak as a residential area reserved for the settlement of British families and officials only. But unknown to most is that the peak district of Cheung Chau had once faced the same destiny.

After the end of the First World War, the government took a fancy to the peak districts at the south of Cheung Chau. Despite the decision being met with strong opposition from two Chinese legislators, the Legislative Council passed the Cheung Chau (Residence) Ordinance in 1919, banning ethnic Chinese from living in the area. To mark the boundaries, the government erected multiple boundary stones, starting from the southwest of Po Yue Wan, stretching to the northeast tip of Nam She Tong and to the St. John Hospital, dividing the island into south and north.

Made of granite, each boundary stone is half a metre high and in the shape of a rectangular pillar with a pointed top. The year and abbreviated title of the Ordinance is carved on every stone. This discriminatory ordinance was only abolished in 1946, 16 years later than the similar rule of Victoria Peak. Sadly, most of the century-old boundary stones can no longer be located.

1950s

留產院
MATERNITY HOMES

島上衣食住行、生活配套一應俱全，不過，有一大件事居民必須離島才能應付——分娩。以往島民會在臨盆前請接生婆，到家中或船上產子。直至第二次世界大戰後人口急增，兩所經政府註冊的私立留產院於五十年代成立，由獲認可的助產士打理，所簽發的證明文件可用作領取出世紙。但隨著公立醫院的婦產服務日漸完善，兩間留產院於七十年代相繼閉門。長洲醫院現不設婦產科，居民必須前往市區待產，不似舊時能真正的「島生島長」。

On Cheung Chau, there is no lack of necessities like food, housing and medical care, except for one service—childbirth. In the past, people would ask midwives to travel to their homes or boats to help. Facing a sharp increase in population during the post-war period, two government-registered private maternity homes were established in the 50s. The facilities were looked after by certified nurse-midwives who could sign documents for the birth certificate application.

As more and more people preferred midwifery services at public hospitals, both maternity homes shut in the 70s. In present-day Cheung Chau, the St. John Hospital does not have an obstetrics and gynecology department. Residents must travel to the city to await delivery. The children of Cheung Chau are no longer born on the island.

1960s

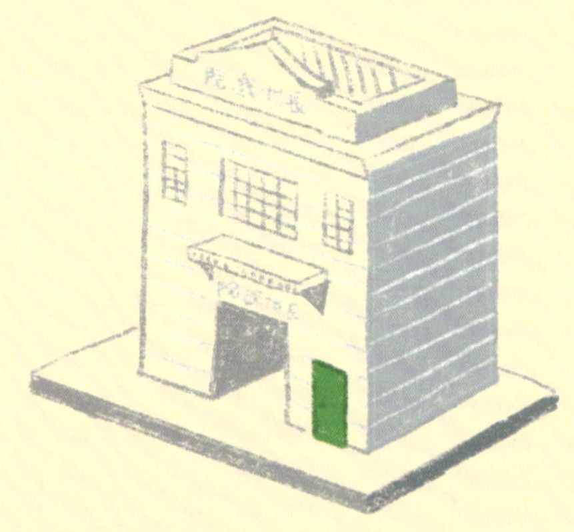

戲院同舟共濟
THE TWO CINEMAS

即使現在長洲有各式文娛康樂設施，但相信不少街坊也希望能在島上享受大銀幕的獨特觀影體驗。事實上，長洲曾經有過兩間電影院。兩層高的長洲戲院建於 1931 年，是繼 1930 年落成的油麻地戲院後，香港第二間電影院，同為戰前僅有的兩間戲院，被列為三級歷史建築。戲院位於香港長洲新興後街，佔地約三萬多平方呎，觀眾席設逾六百個座位，全盛時期常常全院滿座，連通道也擠滿戲迷。戲院外同樣熱鬧，有大量小販擺檔，售賣甘蔗、涼果等小食。走過黑白默片到彩色聲畫年代、服務街坊超過六十個寒暑後，長洲戲院於九十年代初結業，一直荒廢至今。

另一間電影院位於大菜園路，於 1957 年開幕，本稱為金門戲院，後易名為金龍戲院。歇業後已拆卸建為住宅，即現在的金龍花園。聽街坊說，長洲戲院較多西片，而金門則主要播放華語電影。雖現已無從稽考當年上映的劇目，但肯定的是，兩所戲院均心繫長洲。據《華僑日報》報導，1960 年六月上旬颱風瑪麗襲港時，颶風中心更在長洲盤旋，捲起達三層樓高的巨浪，擊沉了一百三十八艘船，令數十名漁民葬身大海，八百餘人無家可歸。兩間戲院見此各辦義映，把當天收入所得悉數撥捐賑災。

Though there are numerous recreational facilities on Cheung Chau, many islanders miss the unique experience of watching films on the silver screen.

Cheung Chau had two cinemas in the past. The first one was the two-storey Cheung Chau Cinema, constructed in 1931. It was the second cinema ever built in Hong Kong, with the first one being the Yau Ma Tei Theater which opened in 1930. As the city's only two cinemas built before the Second World War, they were declared Grade III Historic Buildings.

The Cheung Chau Cinema was located on Sun Hing Back Street. It had a size of 30,000 sq. ft and boasted an auditorium of 600 seats. In its heydays, they always had a full house, even the aisles were packed with people. It was equally lively outside the theatre, where lots of hawkers sold snacks such as sugar cane and dried fruits. From black-and-white silent films to coloured motion pictures, the Cheung Chau Cinema had served the community for over 60 years. It remains a derelict site after it shut in the early 90s.

The other cinema was located on Tai Choi Yuen Road and opened its doors in 1957. Originally called the Dragon Gate Theatre, it was renamed the Golden Dragon Theatre shortly after. The theatre was repurposed into residential buildings called the Kam Lung Garden after it shut.

As many locals recall, the Cheung Chau Theatre mostly showed Western blockbusters, while the Golden Dragon Theatre screened Sinophone films. Regardless of their differences in film selection, both theatres were known to have done a lot for the local community. When Typhoon Mary swept through Hong Kong in 1960, the eye of the storm was centred at Cheung Chau. Great waves with the height of a three-storey building bashed the coastlines and wrecked 138 boats, according to *Overseas Chinese Daily News*. Dozens of fishermen were drowned and over 800 people were rendered homeless. The two cinemas held charity screenings and donated all the proceeds to help the storm-affected islanders.

1970S

移櫻就砌
THE CHERRY BLOSSOMS

賞櫻不一定要到日本，長洲南部也可以一睹櫻花的美態！每逢初春約二月底至三月中，關公忠義亭前的櫻樹便會綻放盛開。關公忠義亭本為關帝廟，因建築外觀才改稱「亭」，亭前的花園種植了十多棵櫻樹，年復年地吸引了不少

攝影發燒友和遊客慕名而至。櫻樹在七十年代由台灣移植來港，屬山櫻品種，開花時全株無葉，花苞細小而密，呈深桃紅色，

Besides travelling all the way to Japan to see cherry blossoms, these stars of springtime can also be found in the southern part of Cheung Chau.

The cherry blossoms in front of the Kwan Kung Pavilion are in full bloom around late February to mid-March. The Kwan Kung Pavilion is a Kwan Tai Temple and was renamed "pavilion" due to its architectural features. More than ten cherry blossom trees attract many photography enthusiasts and tourists to visit the garden every year. The trees, belonging to the Prunus serrulata species, were transported from Taiwan to Hong Kong in the 70s. The bulbs come in small clusters and are magenta in colour.

1990s

香港史上奧運第一金
HONG KONG'S FIRST OLYMPIC GOLD

1996 年 7 月，「風之后」李麗珊為香港摘下史上首面奧運金牌。李麗珊在長洲土生土長，十兄弟姊妹中排行第八，因舅父黎根而培養出對滑浪風帆的興趣，12 歲起學習受訓。她奪金後回到長洲住所，看到接近一萬名居民聚集於碼頭，夾道歡迎她衣錦榮歸，不禁激動落淚。本地動畫《麥兜故事》更以她與黎根作為故事角色，讚揚其發奮向上的精神。「滑浪風帆紀念花園」同年於東灣泳灘旁落成，以紀念這個歷史時刻，並推廣滑浪風帆運動。

In July 1996, windsurfer Lee Lai Shan won the first Olympic gold medal in the history of Hong Kong. Dubbed the "Queen of the Wind", Lee was born and raised on Cheung Chau and is the eighth child amongst ten siblings. She developed her interest in windsurfing thanks to her uncle Lai Gun and started training at 12 years old.

When she returned to Cheung Chau after the historic victory, more than 10,000 people gathered at the pier to welcome her home. Lee, seeing the crowd, was moved to tears. The local animation film *My Life* as *McDull* bases its characters on Lee and Lai as a nod to their spirit of dedication and perseverance. The Windsurfing Memorial at the Tung Wan Beach Garden was unveiled in the same year, commemorating this important moment and promoting windsurfing to the public.

Chapter 02

第二章

Delicacies

食

長洲是個雜姓島，人們帶着各自的生活習慣和文化習俗落戶長洲，同時帶來多元的飲食文化，漁民的海上鮮、粵式茶樓點心、港式茶餐廳……近年，有更多新一代長洲人破舊立新，在島上開設新式餐廳和咖啡店，小小一個島，中西日意泰越……講得出的，幾乎都食得到。食物除了裹腹，更是社區生活之必要，街坊見面不外乎飲飲食食，茶餘飯後打吓牙骹，人與人之間的關係也就在餐桌上漸吃漸濃。

Cheung Chau is an island of mixed origins. Different peoples have brought along their own lifestyles and cultural habits when they came to settle, contributing to a diverse culinary culture that includes fishermen's seafood, Cantonese dim sum, Hong Kong-style *cha chaan teng*, and many more. In recent years, a younger generation of islanders has livened the island's gastronomic scene with new coffee shops and delectable destinations, representing nearly any cuisine imaginable. There is always more to food than fuel. Sharing plates and hanging out over drinks with neighbours are probably some of the best ways to bond.

多多麵
XYB
先選粉麵 後選餸菜
製作需時 耐心等候
麵到請付 謝
東和
招牌麵
WARNING:
嚴禁吸煙
NO SMOKING

多多麵

Dao Dao Noodles

多多麵
人情美味 缺一不可

曾經，車仔麵經營者推着木頭車在街邊擺賣，衛生狀況參差，但勝在又平又快，故被稱為「嗱喳麵」。然而，在長洲有這麼一間車仔麵，一點都不「嗱喳」，反而由湯底、餸料到自家研發的薑蒜辣醬，全都是用心製作，難怪即使是位於遊客罕至的斜路上，每逢周末午市仍然旺場到不得了。

麵檔名為多多麵，以老闆的大仔為名。多多麵的老闆姓蕭，英文名叫 Joby，冬天時一頭灰白中長中分鬈髮，夏天就換上清爽的短髮，偶爾撞見他跟妻子出香港，更會悉心打扮，穿皮褸牛仔褲，七十有一，仍瀟灑有型。

雖然現時備料煮麵等工作都由兩名兒子和幾位老臣子員工主理，但蕭生仍經常在店前坐鎮，除了打點店內大小事務，他最重要的身分是公關：「客人好鐘意見到我哋喺度，有傾偈傾，見到面問一句『近來點呀？』，係唔係都搵啲話題講，好緊要。呢種店香港好少，

譬如你去大家樂點會見到老細？長洲就唔同。」現代術語叫 social，也是人情味之所在。

Joby 廿歲出頭去行船，那是七十年代，當時做船員收入高，三副的月薪有一千多元，相比當時其他行業的四、五百元多一倍有多，即使不用上船，在岸上 stand-by 的月份，公司也會支付半份糧，因此海員是當時的熱門工作。蕭生在船上只待了七個月，就因緣際遇升上三副，隨着貨船走遍大江南北，精通多國語言，日語尤佳。他離職前已是大副，再升上去就是船長，但船員生涯始終漂泊，一出海至少十五個月，為了成家立室，他決定終結十年的海員工作，他打趣地

說：「行船難搵老婆，一行十五至十八個月，鬼等你咩，除非你好英俊瀟灑。」喜歡音樂的他，到每一個城市都必定會逛 CD 舖，多多麵亦有一個小小的唱片架，擺放老闆的心頭好，由搖滾到古巴音樂都有，遇上知音，他會熱心介紹心儀的樂隊。

回到岸上之後，蕭生曾短暫從事絲網印刷，其後在西環開了十年男裝店，及在公正行負責驗船，百足多爪，打滾過後，四十七歲時決定回長洲開車仔麵，「那時幾蚊一個餸，一個麵底嗌幾個餸已經幾十蚊，有得做喎！」當時車仔麵在長洲尚算新鮮事，只有一間早上十一點多就收工的張安記，其他麵檔都是以雲吞麵為主。

初開店時，多多麵由蕭生和妻子打理，現時則交到兩個兒子手上，弟弟 Kelvin 負責幕後工作，每朝早六點三便到店醃好食材，之後回家補眠，再到店幫忙；哥哥阿多十點多上班，主要負責落單、淥麵、計數。除了堂食，還有外賣自取和外送，經常忙到不可開交，街坊在島上大街小巷見到兩兄弟騎著單車「片」過，也見慣不怪。哥哥阿多指一開始接手時，長洲比現時有更多學生，到了中午放飯，麵店外就大排長龍，他要跟時間鬥快，在四十五分鐘時間內做好所有麵，讓同學有時間食。為了爭取時間，在多多落單永遠要先點麵底，麵煮好了，再點配料，如此一來，只要照單執藥，把餸放到麵上就完成，

「我哋賣點係快，個個都係急先過嚟買外賣，外賣等十五分鐘已經覺得好耐。」

光看多多麵的餐牌，未必覺得與坊間的太大分別，但食落口卻大相逕庭，湯底鮮甜，沒有味精，餸料大部分都有加工醃製，如南乳雞翼、冬菇、有點似日式叉燒的咸豬肉等等，弟弟指：「每一樣配料都有自己的味道，唔係就咁淥熟，靠湯底提供味道。」問到最難處理的食材是什麼，兩兄弟竟然說是現在已經無賣的枝竹。原來買回來的枝竹要蒸淋，吹乾，再炸，一批枝竹要整四日，弄得好的枝竹吸汁能力高，非常滋味。而令整碗麵點睛的，必定是自家調製的辣醬，有蒜的香，薑和辣椒的辣，與湯頭的清甜十分匹配。

即使有真材實料，飲食業始終難做，早年長洲食肆不多，競爭尤其激烈。多年前，多多麵曾被人指控重用隔渣後的湯供客人食用，一時間謠言滿天飛，有人加鹽加醋，很多食客信以為真，令麵檔半年來只剩平日的三成客量，最終要整花牌澄清，兩兄弟回想起也感無奈：「我哋自己都係食一樣嘅嘢，有咩可能會咁做？」

現時長洲的飲食版圖比以前更闊也更多元，但遊客始終以打卡為己任，很少人會專程到長洲食一碗車仔麵，但光是長洲島內的街坊熟客，已夠晒忙。近年周末遊客大增，不想出街迫，更多街坊寧願嗌外賣在家吃。每逢周末中午時份，多多的氣氛就緊張起來，但店內眾人臨危不亂，阿多仍然記得哪位熟客要什麼麵底，吃得多辣；弟弟仍然馬不停蹄送外賣；蕭生繼續接聽響個不停的外賣電話，繼續跟客人打牙骹。

美味、人情、速度，一樣不缺，只有多多。

OLDNAVY
1993
HILFIGER JEANS
TOMMY HILFIGER

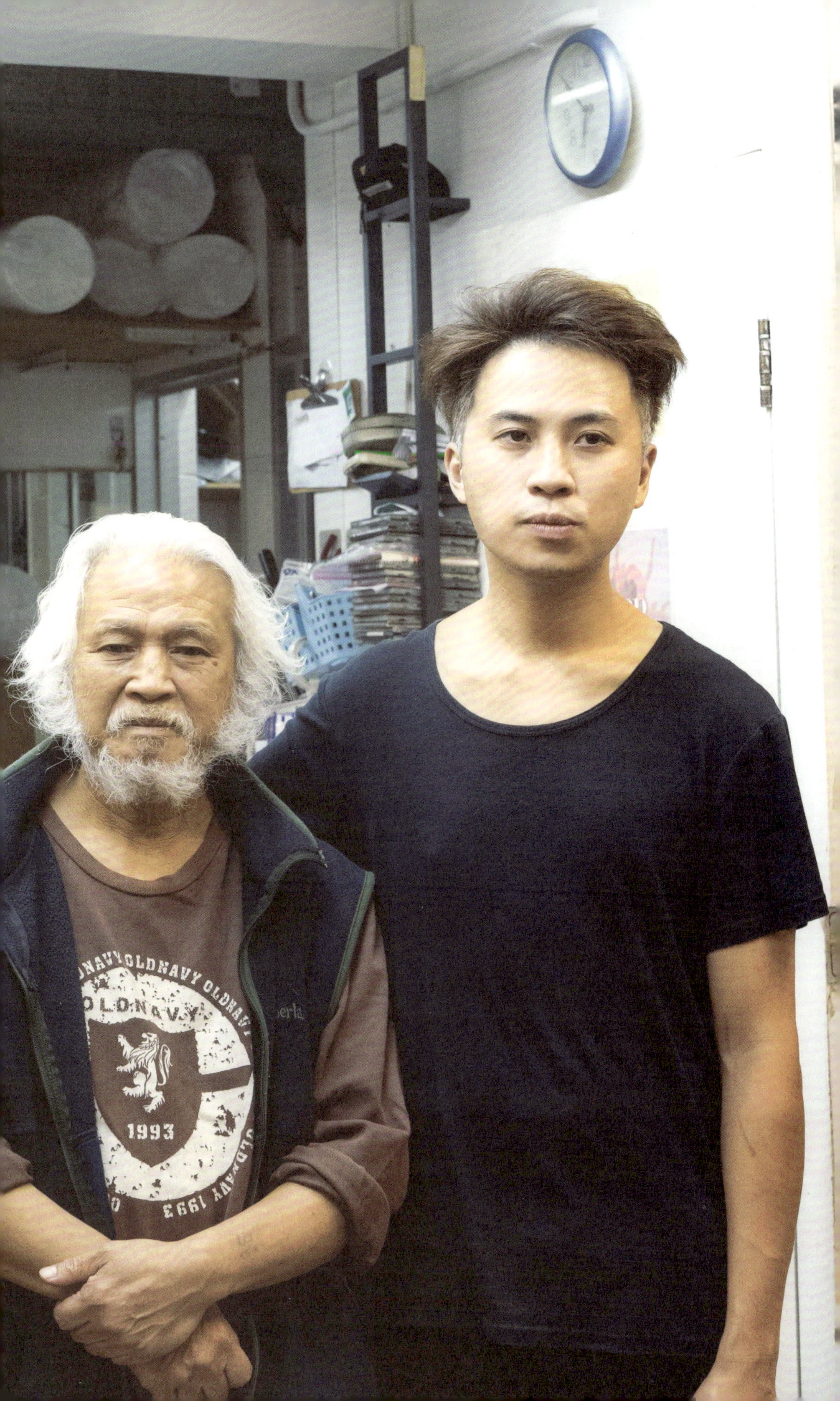
OLDNAVY
1993

Dao Dao Noodles: **PERSONALITY AND DELICACY IN ONE BOWL**

Originating in the 1950s, cart noodles used to be sold by street vendors from wooden carts. Though nicknamed “filthy noodles” because of poor hygiene, their low prices and quick deliveries made the dish a beloved Hong Kong staple.

The cart noodles of Dao Dao are nowhere near “filthy” however. Their soup base, toppings, and homemade ginger garlic spicy sauce are all homemade with love and unique recipes. That’s why the shop always has a full house during lunch hours every weekend, despite its location on a steep road with little foot traffic.

Dao Dao Noodles was named after the eldest son of its owner Joby Siu. Joby wears his grey hair in a mid-length wavy style in the winter and changes it to a fresh, short haircut in the summer. He always puts on his leather jacket and denim jeans whenever he goes to Hong Kong—still stylish and elegant in his 70s.

The work of preparing the ingredients and cooking the noodles is now handled by his two sons and several long-serving staffers, but Joby still spends a lot of time at the shop. His most important role is in public relations, among other chores. “Customers love to see us here. We always try to strike up a conversation,” Joby says. “This type of restaurant is very rare in Hong Kong. Like you will never see the owner at Café de Coral. It is different on Cheung Chau.” What is now called “socialising” is where the human touch lies.

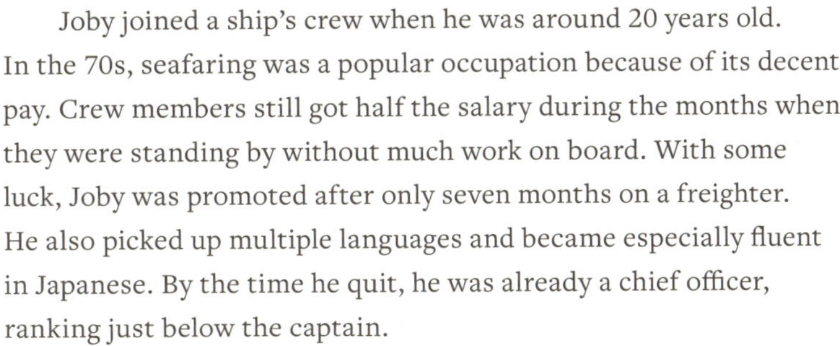

Joby joined a ship's crew when he was around 20 years old. In the 70s, seafaring was a popular occupation because of its decent pay. Crew members still got half the salary during the months when they were standing by without much work on board. With some luck, Joby was promoted after only seven months on a freighter. He also picked up multiple languages and became especially fluent in Japanese. By the time he quit, he was already a chief officer, ranking just below the captain.

A sailor was always on the move, with every trip lasting at least 15 months. Joby, who wanted to start a family, ultimately decided to end his ten years on the sea. "It was difficult for a sailor to find a wife. Every trip lasted 15 to 18 months. Who would wait for you?" He adds, "Unless you are very handsome."

Joby had a habit of buying CDs from record stores in every city he visited. The small rack at Dao Dao Noodles showcases his favourite records. From rock to Cuban music, he is always eager to introduce bands of his choice to other music lovers at the noodle shop.

Joby has kept himself busy after moving back onshore. He worked in silkscreen printing briefly, then ran a menswear shop in Hong Kong Island for ten years. He has also served as a ship inspector for a survey company.

When he was 47, he decided to return to Cheung Chau to open a cart noodle shop. "Back then, the price was a couple of dollars for each topping, and along with the noodle base, each bowl of noodle soup was sold for around HK$30. It was a good business opportunity!" At that time, cart noodles were still something new on Cheung Chau. Only Cheung On Kee, which closed early before noon, sold cart noodles, other stalls mainly offered wonton noodles. The shop was run by Joby and his wife when it first opened.

Now Dao Dao Noodles is in the good hands of their two sons. Kelvin, the younger son who is in charge of food preparation, starts at 6:15 a.m. every morning to marinate the ingredients. He then heads home to catch some sleep before returning to the shop to help. Dao, the elder brother who comes in at 10 a.m., is mainly responsible for taking orders, cooking noodles, and manning the till. Besides dine-in orders, they also do take-outs and deliveries. The brothers are usually extremely busy and often seen flying through alleys on their bikes.

When Dao first took over, there were more students in Cheung Chau, who formed a long queue outside the shop every noon. He needed to race against the clock to dish out all the orders within 45 minutes so that the students had enough time to eat.

To save time, every customer is asked to pick the toppings only after the noodle base is cooked, so that the chef can add them straight on as he listens to the order. "Efficiency is our selling point," Dao stresses. "People come to buy take-out because they're in a hurry, and a 10- to 15-minute wait is already a long time."

Dao Dao Noodles' menu may not look too different from that of other noodle stalls in town, but the major difference lies in its taste. The broth is fresh and flavourful with no MSG. Topping choices range from chicken wings cooked with red-fermented beancurd to braised shiitake mushrooms and sliced ham that tastes like Japanese chashu.

"Every topping must have its own flavour," Kelvin says. "They can't just be blanched and rely on the taste of the broth." Both Kelvin and Dao find dried beancurd sheet (which is no longer on the menu) the hardest ingredient to get right. Each batch takes four days to make because it must be steamed, dried, then fried. The homemade spicy sauce—a blend of garlic, ginger, and fresh chilies—is a perfect match for the umami soup base and takes the noodles to the next level.

The family-run business excels in its food quality, but catering is a tough business after all. Competition was especially fierce in the shop's early days when there were fewer restaurants on the island. Many years ago, Dao Dao Noodles was accused of reusing filtered broth for new orders. The fabricated rumour caused its business to drop by two-thirds for half a year. The brothers still feel helpless as they recall, "We eat the same noodles, why would we ever do that?" The shop needed to make a flower board statement to clarify in the end.

Nowadays, Cheung Chau is home to many more restaurants of different styles and cuisines, but tourists often prefer checking off major attractions to trying out a bowl of cart noodles. The surge of tourists in recent years has prompted locals to order takeout and enjoy at home. Dao Dao Noodles gets busy at noon every weekend, but the operation is never chaotic. Dao always remembers every regular's preferences for noodles and spice level, Kelvin delivers take-outs one after another. Joby takes endless orders on the phone and mingles with customers.

Delicacy, warmth, and speed in one bowl—only at Cheung Chau's Dao Dao.

長洲哨牙刀

Cheung Chau Sourdough

長洲哨牙刀
天神村的麵包師

這個島，看來與很多其他小島一樣，大街小巷都是踢拖短褲的人，人們衝忙有時，散漫有時，以與市區不同步的調子生活著。長洲哨牙刀(Cheung Chau Sourdough) 的 Wallace 總稱這裡為《IQ 博士》中的「天神村」，他隨口數出這島上的奇人異士：某個大叔是七星螳螂拳的高手、某個阿伯是形意拳的全國副會長、某間茶號創辦人是熟普洱第一人……而他，是這條村裡的「麵包師」。

Wallace 早年曾跟隨父親在內地設廠，製作奢華手袋，又造過鬚刨，但他不樂於把生命交給機器，依賴其他地方的人力物力去生產，反而想嘗試用自己的一對手去過活，於是轉行從事攝影，並於 2008 年搬到長洲居住，一住便十二年，他說：「長洲是很有人氣的地方，沒有太多大財團進駐，很多小店仍生存到，人們亦更加寬容。」他又指，長洲就如香港的縮影，一程船便與中環連接，生活機能齊備，有「市中心」，有大自說，「步行距離已有八個沙灘！」他閒時除了耍太極、行椿，就是釣魚、種植，或心血來潮跟朋友去秘灘自建熱石桑拿。

初到長洲，本想靠攝影維生，同時開始自學做酸種麵包，誰不知後者漸漸成為他的重心。麵包對他有種莫名的吸引力：「麵包是一個生命體，做一個麵包如見證由生到死。」麵包有生命，酸種尤甚。用麵粉和水混合發酵而成的酸種，如同麵包的心臟，溫度和時間控制不同，它便會死亡，Wallace 坦言自己失敗過無數次，扔棄過幾十斤麵糰，但照顧得妥當，它可一直存活。他現時用的酸種已經養了超過三年，要養活它們，每隔十小時便「餵飼」麵粉和水，經年累月後，它們終成為能夠適應長洲氣侯和環境的在地酸種。

全盛時期 Wallace 一星期約做三十至五十條包，分別有全麥和原味法包和意大利拖鞋包，偶爾興起研發新包，如有只在廿四節氣才焗製的麵包。他大部分客人為島上的外國人，也有愈來愈多的本地支持者，甚至衝出長洲，在市區的小店寄賣。麵包出爐，稍涼後，他便用紙或麵包布包着，再用咸水草綁起，附上一張像單據般、印有麵包品種的紙條，設計用心。他盡可能把麵包送到家門，與客人交流，每次包送到手上還是溫熱的。幾年前，他搬到一個新的工房，外面有棵大樹，他曾與友人合辦「長洲芝」，以低廉價格搜羅外國好芝士，每次貨到，便大伙兒聚在樹下開，開幾枝酒，切些芝士麵包，正如 Wallace 所說，做麵包只是第一步：「我希望用麵包去建立人與人之間的關係。」最近，他投放更多心力開班教整包，在長洲以包會友。

Cheung Chau Sourdough: **THE BAKER AND THE VILLAGERS**

Like many other outlying islands, Cheung Chau is filled with people walking around in flip-flops and shorts. Locals live at a different pace from the city dwellers. But Wallace of Cheung Chau Sourdough always likens the island to the Penguin Village—the fictional town in the Japanese manga series Dr. Slump. He casually recounts the strange and peculiar figures on the island: this uncle is a Seven-Star Praying Mantis Boxing master, another is the national vice-chairperson of Xing Yi Quan, a tea shop founder who invented the technique of ripe pu'er tea fermentation, and many more. Then there is Wallace, the village's baker.

Wallace spent his early days managing a factory with his father in Mainland China. They had manufactured luxury handbags, as well as electric shavers, but he didn't want to spend his life with machines. Instead, he wanted to use his own hands to make a living, so he changed track to become a photographer and moved to Cheung Chau in 2008.

"Cheung Chau is a lively place. Not too many corporations have gotten in here, so many independent shops can still survive, and people are also more forgiving," says Wallace. He also sees the island as a miniature of Hong Kong: it is only one ferry ride away from Central; it has all kinds of amenities, a "downtown" and access to nature. "There are eight beaches within walking distance!"

When he is not practising tai chi or standing meditation in his spare time, he would be fishing, gardening or building a hot rock sauna on a secret beach with his friends.

Wallace planned to earn a living with photography when he first moved to Cheung Chau. That was also when he self-taught how to make sourdough bread, which over time became his focus. "Bread is a living thing, it's like witnessing the circle of life when you make bread." All breads are alive, especially sourdough. Born of a fermented mixture of flour and water, the sourdough starter is like a bread's heart, which dies without the right temperature or time control.

Wallace admits that he has failed numerous times, throwing away kilos after kilos of dough. But if it is well taken care of, the starter can keep on living. The starters he is currently using are over three years old. They must be fed with flour and water every other ten hours to stay alive. Over the years, the starters have finally adjusted to Cheung Chau's climate and environment.

Wallace can make around 30 to 50 loaves of bread per week, mostly whole wheat and regular baguettes, as well as ciabattas. At times, he experiments with new varieties, such as flavours specific to the changing seasons. Most of his clients are expats living on the island, but he also has some local supporters. Whenever a batch of freshly baked bread is ready, he lets it cool down slightly before wrapping each order with paper or cloth, then typing it up with a grass cord and attaching a note that details the bread type. He endeavours to deliver the still-warm orders to each household himself and catch up with his clients.

As Wallace stresses, bread-making is just the first step. "I hope to connect with others through bread."

Heima Heima

Heima Heima
在海邊的第二個家

長洲大概分了東西兩邊，渡輪碼頭所在的東邊是熱鬧的市中心，西邊是較為寧靜的一隅，只有零星店舖，東、西邊像兩個世界。Heima Heima 的店主 Clara 說，自己的生活也像分開了兩個世界，一邊是開店（上班）的日子，在長洲，另一邊是無需開店的日子，在市區。

Clara 是少數非長洲居民，卻特地到長洲開店的人。四年前，她和丈夫 Brian 在西灣開設咖啡店，取名 Heima Heima，是冰島文「家」的意思。這小店也的確像二人的第二個家，兩口子一起構想和設計店內的裝潢：門的側邊開一隻看到海的大大的窗，桌上放些用心物色的器物和擺設，播喜歡的音樂（當然包括二人喜歡的冰島樂隊 Sigur Rós），研發新的甜點，尋找心儀的本地烘焙咖啡豆，它是打開門做生意的咖啡店，也是二人生活的一部分。

選擇長洲，純粹出於緣分，「這是我和丈夫第一次約會的地方。」Clara 甜絲絲地說。Brian 喜歡攝影和飲咖啡，拍拖節目不外乎去咖啡店，以及到離島和郊外。她回想起開店時的長洲，「長洲感覺在地一點，有不少老店，餐廳種類也不多，主要以茶餐廳為主。長洲雖然有很多居民，但沒有一間有特色的咖啡店。」尤其是以民居為主的西灣，當時更只有一、兩間士多，誰也沒有想到 Clara 和 Brian 竟在這

裡落戶。「當時地產經紀也很驚訝，他說『呢度無人嚟喎！』但我跟他說：『我一個人在這裡都可以。』」她笑言自己是白羊座性格，「做咗先算。」隨後西園營地和酒吧餐廳海盜灣先後開業，島的西邊也漸漸熱鬧起來。而長洲全島也陸續開設多間年輕咖啡店，每逢假日不少人慕名而至。

小店初期一周開足六日，但人流不多，Clara 亦曾為之擔心，但四年後的今日，一星期多數只開三日，客人卻絡繹不絕，雖然與當初理想中的海邊靜好咖啡店的氛圍有出入，但跟以往在市區打工的生活相比，她更享受開店的自在：「開店之後，我好像變懶了（笑）。以前打工會很大壓力，現在開店雖也有壓力，但至少可以自己做決定，自己控制，個人舒服了很多。」

也有些東西是 Clara 多年來仍然非常享受的，她每逢開店日，都會由碼頭沿海邊踩單車到西灣，天氣好的時侯，吹着微風，看粼粼波光，「那風景我看了這麼多遍，仍然覺得很美。」她亦記得在開店的第二日，一群在長洲開小店的年輕店主一起去光顧，之後更變成好友。這分情誼，大概是連鄰居也不認識的市區生活難以比擬的。

Today's Special
1. Lime & Honey Cheesecake
青檸蜂蜜芝士蛋糕 $48
2. Lychee Oolong Tea Roll Cake
$48
3. Japan Mikan Roll Cake
$48
a. Iced Mango & Lemon Soda
$40
b. Iced Apple Earl Grey Tea
$40
c. Oolong Tea Latte
$36/$40 Iced
d. Cold Brew Tea (Oolong)
$48
e. Black Bean Tea (Pot)
$48
ORDER HERE
heima heima

Heima Heima: **A SECOND HOME BY THE SEA**

To Cheung Chau natives, the east and the west of the island resemble two separate worlds. On the east where the public pier is the lively downtown, while the west is quieter with fewer stores. Clara too finds herself travelling between two worlds since the launch of Heima Heima in 2016—running her Nordic-style café on Cheung Chau three to four days a week and living in Hong Kong on the other days.

Clara is one of the very few business owners who do not live on the island. Heima means 'home' in Icelandic. Indeed, the cozy café is the second home of Clara and her husband Brian, who conceptualised and designed its interiors from scratch. With their favourite music (including, of course, the Icelandic band Sigur Rós) playing in the air, the couple experiment with dessert recipes and try out different coffee beans roasted in town. To Clara and Brian, the café is more than a business, it is part of their lives.

Cheung Chau was a coincidental choice. "This is where my husband and I had our first date," Clara says. Brian is a photography and coffee lover. When the two were dating, they frequented cafés, the countryside, and outlying islands. "When we first opened the shop, Cheung Chau was a down-to-earth island with plenty of old businesses and a limited variety of restaurants," Clara recalls. "Despite being inhabited by many, there wasn't a decent coffee shop."

Sai Wan, in particular, only had one to two tuck shops, as the area was mostly residential. Nobody would have expected Clara and Brian's choice of location. "The real estate agent was taken by surprise and confessed there weren't any visitors here. But I told him that I would be alright even with being here by myself." A self-described Aries, Clara simply went ahead with the venture. Following the openings of Sai Yuen Camping Adventure Park and Pirate Bay next door in subsequent years, the west of Cheung Chau became more dynamic. Three to four younger cafés also took root in other parts of the island, attracting a wider crowd during the holidays.

Heima Heima initially opened six days a week and the low traffic of customers did worry Clara. Now after four years, the café only opens three to four days a week but is always packed with visitors. While it's not exactly the ideal vibe she envisioned for a quiet seaside café, Clara prefers the freedom that comes with Heima Heima to her previous day job in the city. "I think I've become more laid-back," Clara laughs. "I was stressed out when I was working for others in the past. Running a café comes with pressure too, but at least I can make my own decisions and be in control. I feel so much more relaxed."

Four years on, Clara still enjoys cycling along the promenade from the pier to Sai Wan when the weather is nice, taking in the soft breeze and shimmering waters. "No matter how many times I see that view, I still find it beautiful." She also holds dear the friendship with other young Cheung Chau store owners, developed after they visited Heima Heima on the second day of its opening. Such bonding is few and far between in the urban jungle, where neighbours tend to remain strangers.

6 8
F E

海盜灣

Pirate Bay

海盜灣
西灣的街坊客廳

（已於 2023 年結業）

海盜灣店外的三把太陽傘下，放著兩台薄餅專用的平底煎鍋，來自數年前長洲海傍街的法式可麗餅車仔檔，檔主匆匆離港便把電爐暫存於朋友家，來到西灣才重見天日，薄餅的甜香總在周末引來人龍。

甫進店，左面角落的天花垂著灰色水晶吊燈，來自法國五月藝術節的活動，紅色牆上掛着巴黎的地鐵路綫圖。右面則吊著四個圓蒸籠和兩個竹篾燈籠，分別漆著「合境平安」和「天地父母」的紅字，是每年太平清醮的民俗工藝品，暖和的燈光下是一幅剛勁遒媚的書法，寫著《海盜的後裔》的歌詞，下款署名「源良」。小店招牌上的「海盜灣」三字，亦是出自著名填詞人潘源良之手。

歌唱家 Priscilla 和來自巴黎的丈夫 David 於 2009 年搬到長洲。David 完成掏盡十年心血的博士論文後惘然若失，正巧家門前的茶餐廳找人接手，便從一個研究五四運動的歷史學者，搖身一變成法國大廚。

「不過其實，我們只是把家中客廳搬了過來。」Priscilla 指指吧枱前疊滿書的紅酒木箱說：「所有看不明的學術書，全都是他的。」

海盜灣的確有令人回到家的感覺，不論是廚房外長開的麻雀枱，還是細心健談的女主人和風趣幽默的男主人。餐廳除了供應 David 的自家製香腸、法式肝醬、長棍麵包等美食，還會舉辦周五免費電影

會、不定期的 Open Mic 棟篤唱等文化聚會，更會借出場地予純素廚師設宴，甚至騰出空間給街坊暫放雜物。

這間張保仔洞旁的小店，實質是一間好客的社區中心。

「我們甚至連托兒都不放過，哈！」新冠肺炎壓境，全港學校停課，Priscilla 聽到街坊說全天候照顧孩子如「困獸鬥」，便開設下午茶卡通放映會，令家長們可以喘喘氣。

街坊也待小店如家，下雨天前會主動幫忙收下綁好門外的太陽傘。「不單是幫我們手，更是守望相助，大家都不想有人受傷，尤其這邊住了比較多老人家。」

海盜灣自 2018 年農曆年假開業後，即使遠在西灣這個天然避風塘，仍同見證著香港近年的風風浪浪。

「每年都總會發生一些令人措手不及的事。前年登革熱、上年社會動盪、今年肺炎肆虐，重挫了長洲、甚至全港的旅遊業。既然做生意不免要面對種種不穩定，那不如先尋歡作樂，自己玩得開心也很緊要。」一頭爽朗短髮的 Priscilla 笑笑說。

Pirate Bay: THE NEIGHBOURHOOD'S LIVING ROOM

(Permanently closed in Dec 2023)

In the outdoor seating of Pirate Bay stands a trolley with two crêpe makers from a stall on Praya Street. The original owner left them at a friend's rooftop before leaving Hong Kong, before they were given a second chance to shine in Sai Wan. The enticing aroma of French crêpes has attracted so many, especially weekend visitors, to this cozy harbour-front bar and restaurant.

Right at the entrance of the restaurant are a chandelier and a poster of a Parisian metro map. On the other side of the ceiling hangs several Chinese bamboo steam baskets and lanterns from the annual Da Jiu Festival. Warm lights illuminate a work of Chinese calligraphy quoting lyrics from "The Pirate's Offspring", signed by renowned lyricist Calvin Poon. Poon also lent his calligraphy to Pirate Bay for its storefront sign.

Classical opera singer Priscilla moved to Cheung Chau in 2009 with David, her husband from Paris. Originally a history scholar with a focus on the May Fourth Movement, David was at a loss after finishing his Ph.D. thesis, to which he had devoted a decade of his life. Coincidentally, a cha chaan teng right across the couple's home was looking to sell at the time. And just like that, David pivoted and became a chef.

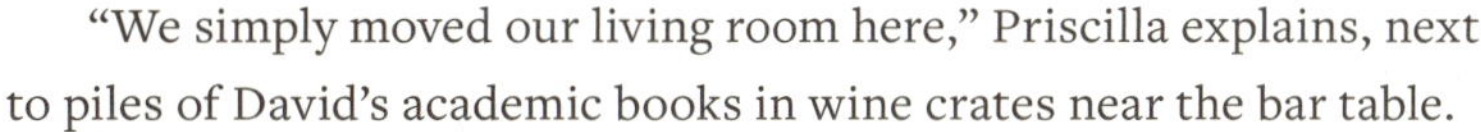

"We simply moved our living room here," Priscilla explains, next to piles of David's academic books in wine crates near the bar table.

Pirate Bay reminds people of home, with its mahjong table outside of the kitchen, a thoughtful and gregarious host, and a cheery chef with the best sense of humour. Besides serving classics such as David's homemade sausages, liver pâté and baguettes, the restaurant has held various events such as free movie nights on Fridays and occasional open mics. They even lend the space to a vegan chef for hosting dinners and to villagers who are looking for temporary storage. This French bistro near the Cheung Po Tsai Cave is indeed a community centre in disguise.

"We're even doing daycare!" Priscilla says. As schools around Hong Kong shut down due to COVID-19, Priscilla heard some neighbours lament the ordeal of full-time childcare. She then organised tea-time cartoon screenings so that parents could drop their kids off for a breather.

Locals also treat Pirate Bay like their own home. They would help secure the outdoor umbrellas before rainy days so that passersby wouldn't get hurt. Priscilla describes their helping hand as a form of communal support, which is especially valuable as many seniors live in the neighbourhood.

Since its opening back in 2018, Pirate Bay has been witnessing the ups and downs of Hong Kong even as the owners enjoy relative peace in the far-away Sai Wan. "Something unexpected happens every year," Priscilla says. "It was Dengue fever the year before last, followed by social unrest, and then we've got Covid this year, which has dealt a huge blow to Cheung Chau and the tourism industry in general."

"Given that we have no choice but to face all kinds of uncertainties in business, it's more important to find joy in life for ourselves and have fun first and foremost."

長洲大新街67號地下
P.V.C. CABLE
請
按鐘
買茶
全长洲

百年平安茶

Tea For A Century Of Health

巷仔內的百年平安茶
「買茶：按玲」

天時暑熱，當遊客都循指定路線大汗疊細汗吃大魚蛋、糯米糍，長洲人則施施然鑽進一條隱蔽的小巷，飲一杯清熱解渴的涼茶，放低幾蚊，換來一口清涼。

說的是劉太經營的「百年平安茶」。雖說她的檔口開在後巷，但巷口有個醒目的招牌招徠，紅紅黃黃的 banner，大大隻寫上「本島最老涼茶舖」，好不霸氣。往巷子裡那亮着黃燈的地方走，便是劉太和丈夫經營了二十多年的涼茶檔。

檔口雖小，但設計非常別緻，黃燈的源頭是一盞用涼茶紙杯製成的吊燈，劉太指在巷口也有另一盞紙杯燈，入黑後見它亮著就代表仍在開舖，無光就是收工了，以免人們走進巷子才發覺無開門，白行一趟。這些貼心的設計都是出自劉生之手，包括桌上一個門鈴，旁邊寫上「買茶：按玲」，當劉太不在店面時客人可按鈴示意，喜歡開玩笑的劉太說：「我常取笑他之前一定有個叫阿玲的女友，念念不忘，所以寫錯字，把『鈴』寫了做『玲』。」

年屆七十的劉太在長洲出世，她指當時媽媽沒有到醫院生，由接生婆在家接生，所以連出世紙也沒有。她小時候父母在長洲開米舖，她自小幫家裡砍柴和送米，婚後隨丈夫搬出九龍城，開士多維生，住了十年八年，及後搬回長洲開茶餐廳，又做了十年八年。對比起市區，她更喜歡長洲空氣好，又有人情味，「去飲茶或街市買餸都可以跟人聊天，好多傷傾，在九龍時，連住在隔壁那個人都不認識。」

直到二十多年前，一個在長洲開涼茶店的八十多歲婆婆打算退休專心湊孫，於是劉太用幾萬蚊向婆婆買下秘方，接手茶檔。涼茶檔獨賣四味：廿四味、五花茶、銀菊露，以及紫背天葵，有杯裝和支裝，喜歡的也可以兩溝。訪問期間，客人不絕，男女老幼都有，據說上一手涼茶婆婆以前在澳門做中醫，所以涼茶特別有效，尤其是廿四味，煲足八、九小時，不少人喉嚨痛、感冒、生痱滋都會飲一杯。

劉太現時每朝五點幾便起身煲茶，每日煲幾十枝，去東灣游個水或踩單車，再飲個茶便開檔，但問她自己喜歡像哪一款，她耍手擰頭：「我款款都唔鍾意，聞得太多，聞到個鼻都唔知咩嚟啦！」她直言煲涼茶很辛苦，無意把秘方和檔口再傳下去。

訪問完結前，攝影師跟劉太拍照，她拿起一杯全島最老涼茶，對鏡頭笑得開懷，攝影師讚她很有自信，鬼馬的她贈我們一句金句：「梗係啦！無自信點做人！」

茶·巷内

前一步
百年
平安茶
(小樽)
(大樽)
杯 10
2杯 19
3杯 25
10
9
8
長洲
最老之
請
一時開

Baak Nin Ping On Cha: **A CENTURY-OLD HERBAL TEA DOWN THE ALLEY**

In the searing Cheung Chau heat, as tourists flock to snack stalls for giant fishballs and mango mochi, locals would slip into a hidden alley for a cup of refreshing Chinese herbal tea.

The stall named "Tea For A Century Of Health" has a bright red and yellow banner that boasts its status as the island's oldest herbal tea business. The tiny space is impeccably designed by Mr. Lau. A chandelier made from paper cups illuminates the space with a warm yellow glow. Another cup lamp on the other end of the alley tells customers when it's open for business, so that they won't walk all the way after closing time. On the desk is a doorbell with a sign that says "Ring this bell for tea", for customers to call for Mrs. Lau when she is not manning the stall.

The 70-year-old Mrs. Lau was born on Cheung Chau. Her mother delivered at home with a midwife's help, so she never got a birth certificate. As her parents owned a rice store on the island, she grew up axing firewood and delivering rice. She moved out to Kowloon City to run a small store after getting married.

A decade later, Mrs. Lau returned to Cheung Chau and ran a cha chaan teng, as she missed the fresh air and an unmistakable sense of community on the island. "Here you can always find someone to chat with, whether at a dim sum place or the wet market. And there're always lots of things to talk about." Mrs. Lau adds, "I didn't even know my next-door neighbours when I lived in Kowloon."

Around 20 years ago, an 80-year-old islander decided to retire from the herbal tea trade. Mrs. Lau then bought her secret recipes and took over the business. She only sells four types of tea, available in cups or bottles. The shop is frequented by customers of all ages. The original owner is believed to have practised traditional Chinese medicine in Macau, hence her recipes were especially effective. A regulars favourite is the 24 Flavours tea, brewed for up to nine hours at the stall. Many islanders with sore throats and cold symptoms would stop by for a quick fix.

Mrs. Lau always gets up at 5 a.m. to start the day with a swim or a bike ride in Tung Wan, before opening the stall for business. But she can't name a favourite. "I don't like any of them. I've been smelling them too much to even tell which is which!" Mrs. Lau confesses that making Chinese herbal tea is hard work, and that she has no intention to pass the secret recipes or the business on to anyone.

Mrs. Lau beams as she proudly holds a cup of Cheung Chau's oldest herbal tea for portrait shots. The playful and exuberant octogenarian says: "How can you live without confidence!"

CAFFESIS

耐人尋味

Noi Yan Cham Mei

長洲人的西餐廳 耐人尋味
阿怡：**問自己可以去到幾盡？**

（已於 2021 年結業）

「喂，耐人尋味。A、C、G 餐都賣晒啦。外賣要等一個鐘，你 O 唔 OK？」樓面的侍應在電話那頭說。那邊廂，廚師的手也沒一秒停下，炸薯條、焗 Pizza、炒意粉、出飲料，烽烽火火。餐廳外排隊的客人猶豫着點哪款招牌菜式，哪怕等上半個到一個鐘也在所不計。耐人尋味結業前的這幾天，客人和員工都豁了出去，以一場精彩的「冧檔」，為餐廳畫上句號。

阿怡入行做飲食，多少跟父親有關。父親做雲吞麵起家，最初在碼頭擺車仔檔，做到街知巷聞，幾蚊一碗雲吞麵，賣到養起成頭家，靠的是對食物的執著，她讚嘆道：「老豆係唯一一個，在我心目中擁有極度崇高位置的人，他對食物的堅持，令我也會撫心自問自己做不做到他的程度。有一段時間，市面上興起十蚊雲吞麵，大家追求平靚正，用急凍肉和蝦，不追求新鮮，但我老豆賣十四蚊一碗，因他堅持每日到街市買豬肉手切，蝦一定是街市一擔擔買回來自己剝，他也不用大地魚粉，而用大地魚乾，烤到燶和焦之間，再自己炒芝麻，古法研磨成粉才用來做雲吞餡。」阿怡講起八十年代的長洲碼頭宵夜檔，檔檔都水準超班，做到有聲有色。

到中五畢業後，雖然老豆不願女兒做飲食，但在中學老師幫忙之下，阿怡修讀酒店相關課程，並於灣仔世紀酒店實習，當時阿怡是唯一一個未畢業就已有「大佬」（主廚）邀請做長工的同學，於是她就順勢輟學，正式入行做廚房。那年她十八歲。之後她又到過不同酒店工作，輾轉去了一間五星級大酒店，見盡當中的勾心鬥角，她忍不住

夾雜流利的粗口說：「上班試過被上司D（罵）到喊，喊L住做，一路捱，就算有大佬睇你，其他人不會輕易讓你上位。我以前唔講粗口，但到後來，粗口已成為我身體一部分！」

於是她決定辭職回長洲開店，她稱之為耐人尋味1.0，最初是車仔早餐檔，隨後入舖，父親也落場幫忙，但開業一年後，種種原因令她自感無籌碼再經營下去，便決定結業。阿怡於是重新奔走於不同廚房，但她由大酒店內的小員工，變成獨當一面的主廚。她曾為位於大坑的新餐廳由零開始設計餐單，主打有港式元素的西餐，蔥油海膽、八珍甜醋豬扒包等都是她的得意之作。當時她從來沒想過會有耐人2.0。

神推鬼𢫏之下，阿怡決定回長洲再試一次耐人尋味。比起十年前，阿怡自問戰鬥力增強了，但壓力也更大。她曾聽過不少難聽的話：「失敗過一次仲嚟？!」一開始壓力非常大，一再把自己推到極限。「行外人見到餐牌只得一頁，可能覺得『咁少嘢食嘅？』，但同行都問我：你一個人點做呀？」加上堅持每星期轉菜單，除了考創意，也考驗組織能力：星期三訂貨，星期四清雪櫃，星期五出外買貨，放假構思新餐單，每一項都要計算。雖則耐人只做晚市，更選擇旺場的星期五休息，但其實阿怡每晚凌晨才回家，三年半來如是，「我每日都問自己，可以去到幾盡？」

要領略耐人尋味是一間怎樣的餐廳，再多的形容也不及看它的餐牌來得直接：每星期有七個套餐，有沙律／餐湯、主菜，和飲品，主菜每星期轉一次，這星期有腐乳意粉，下星期是台式手撕雞飯、海膽意粉、泡菜汁意粉、蔥油帶子、燒鴨薄餅……阿怡擅於把中西式食材共冶一爐，而且全都出奇地夾！她不禁自讚一下：「耐人尋味這名字改得好出色，這意味著有空間去試。」

然而，阿怡總說：「我唔鍾意煮嘢食！」鍾意與否是一回事，對待食物的用心和紮實的功架卻騙不了人。意粉炒得有鑊氣，醬汁香濃惹味，炸物鬆脆香口，難怪不少街坊都是熟客，她笑言，一開頭不被看好，現時「門口成地眼鏡碎」。

直到近五、六年前，長洲的飲食版圖仍以茶餐廳和海鮮餐廳為主，到了近年才出現變化，「島二代」和「島三代」開設新式餐廳，日、韓、意大利、法國菜都不缺，為島民提供更多元的選擇。阿怡笑稱耐人尋味是間長洲式的西餐廳，「少少西，唔係十分西」，因餐廳沒有大部分人所期望的西餐模樣：有扒鋸，百幾蚊有湯有主菜有飲品，最好送埋甜品。與其被這框架框住，不如索性打破中西日韓法意餐的邊界，只要做得好食的，就是好餐。餐廳結業後，她開設耐人尋味工作室，教人做迷你黏土食物模型，認真「造假」。

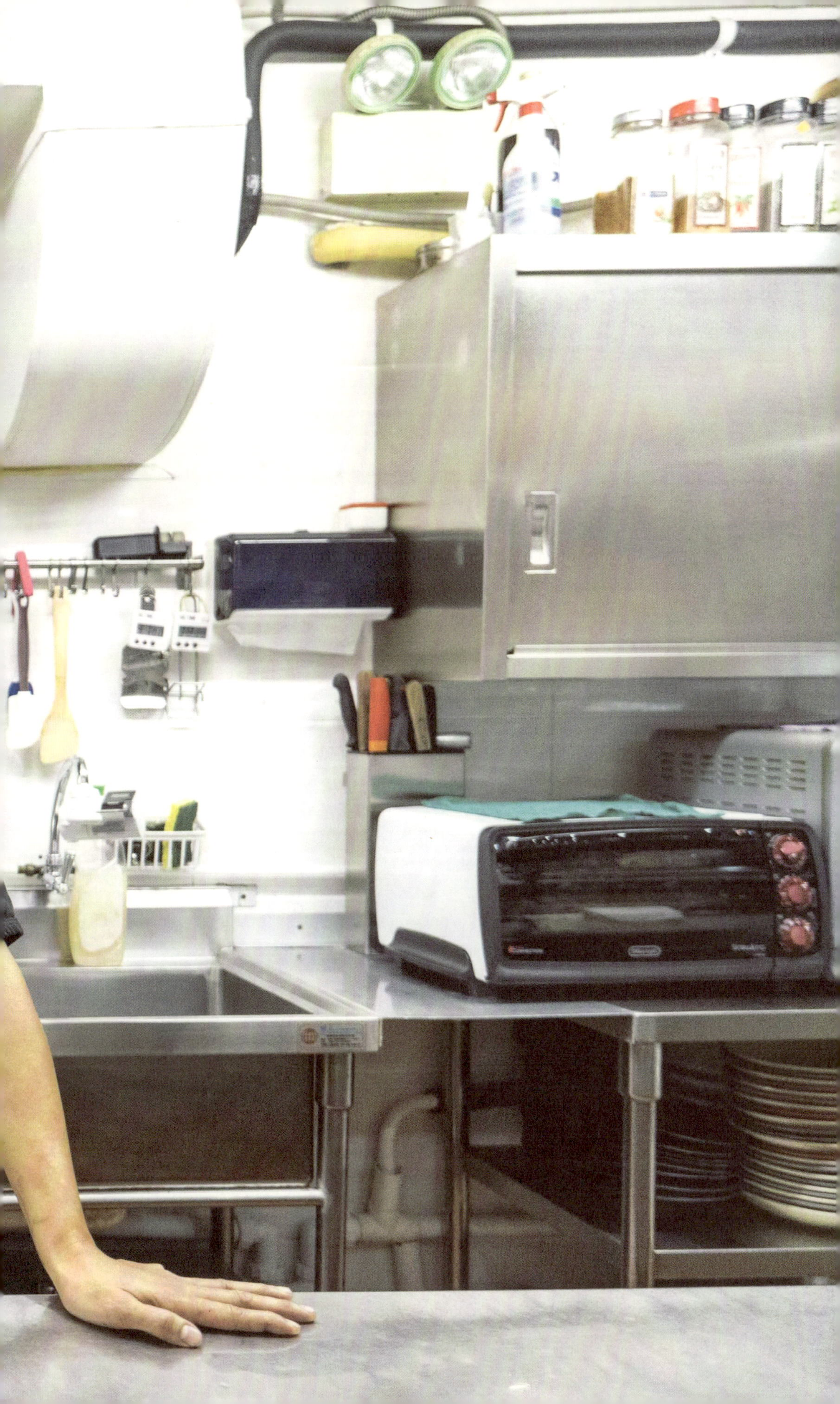

Noi Yan Cham Mei: **PUSHING THE BOUNDARIES OF FUSION CUISINE**

(Closed in 2021)

"Hello! Sets A, C, and G are sold out. Take-out is an hour's wait, are you alright with that?" says the waiter on the phone. Meanwhile in the heated kitchen, the chef juggles between frying fries, baking pizzas, cooking pasta, and making drinks. Locals, who have been queueing outside for almost an hour, have a hard time choosing between signature dishes.

Over the last days of the much-loved bistro, the customers and the staff have been going all out, marking its closure with overwhelming orders.

What brought Yee to the catering industry is more or less related to her father. He used to run a hugely popular wonton noodle stall at the pier. Selling wonton noodles for a few bucks a bowl brought home the bread for the family, and the secret to success was the commitment to food quality. "My dad is the only person that holds a special position in my heart. I honestly cannot match him in his commitment to food," Yee says.

For a long time, HK$10 wonton noodle soup had reigned the market, but her dad refused to follow the trend. "People who valued cheap prices over freshness turned to frozen meat and shrimp. But my dad still sold his noodles at HK$14 a bowl, because he insisted on buying pork and shrimp from the wet market every day and chopped them by hand." Yee's father never used dried flounder fish powder either, but only dried founder fish that he grilled to the perfect state of golden char. He also toasted the sesames himself before grinding them into powder—the traditional way—for the fillings. That's why his wonton noodles remained a strong contender in the exceptionally vibrant night food scene at the Cheung Chau pier in the 80s.

Though her father didn't want her to join the catering business, Yee enrolled in a hospitality course after high school and interned at the Century Hong Kong Hotel in Wan Chai. As the only student who was offered a permanent contract by the head chef before

graduation, she dropped out of school to launch her career in the kitchen at the age of 18. She then went on to work for several other hotels and eventually joined a five-star hotel and witnessed all the power play behind the scenes. "I had been told off by my boss during work and I worked while fucking crying," she can't help but swear. "It was tough. Even if someone higher up had your back, others wouldn't go easy on your promotion. I never cursed before but swearing has become part of me from then on."

So she quit and started her own eatery on Cheung Chau, which she called *Noi yan cham mei* 1.0. What began as a breakfast stall was later moved into a shop. Her father also helped on the floor. One year later, various reasons led Yee to feel that she no longer had what it took to continue, so she decided to shut the business.

Yee then worked in different kitchens again, but her role changed from being a small potato in a big hotel to becoming a chef of her own. She created menus from scratch for a new restaurant in Tai Hang, featuring Hong Kong-style Western cuisine. Sea urchin with scallion oil and pork chop bun with Pat Chun sweetened vinaigrette are among her signature dishes.

Almost out of the blue, Yee decided to return to Cheung Chau and give *Noi yan cham mei* another try after ten years. The fighter has heard harsh words like "why try again when you've already failed once?" The pressure was extremely high in the beginning, and Yee pushed herself to the limit once again. "People might see the one-page menu and think, 'How come there are so few options?' But my peers all questioned how I could manage all that on my own."

Yee also insisted on changing the menu every week, which not only put her creativity to the test, but also her organisational skills—placing food orders on Wednesdays, clearing out the fridges on Thursdays, shopping for other ingredients on Fridays, designing new menus on day-offs. Although the restaurant only served dinners and closed every Friday, Yee always went home after midnight for the last few years. "I asked myself every day: How far could I go?"

There is no better way to understand what kind of a restaurant Yee ran than by looking at its menu: seven set dinners a week, served with a drink, and a salad or soup. The main courses changed weekly, pasta with fermented tofu for one week, Taiwanese-style hand-shredded chicken for the next. Sea urchin pasta, pasta with kimchi sauce, scallops in scallion oil, roast duck pizza... Yee is an expert in fusing Chinese and Western ingredients to create surprisingly matching flavours. "*Noi yan cham mei* is a good name, it means that there's always room for experiment."

Yee may always say "I don't like cooking!", but her care for food and solid skills are unmistakable. The stir-fried pasta has a smoky aroma, the sauce is rich and flavourful... no wonder many regulars are locals. She jokes that most people looked down on her at first, but now she has proven them wrong.

Cheung Chau's restaurant scene was mostly dominated by cha chaan tengs and seafood restaurants until five or six years ago when the second- and third-generation islanders began to open new spots serving Japanese, Korean, Italian and French cuisines. Yee calls *Noi yan cham mei* a Cheung Chau-style Western restaurant: "A bit Western, but not entirely so". Neither a steakhouse nor a fine-dining restaurant, Yee strives to break different culinary boundaries. Anything goes, as long as it tastes good.

Yee now runs an arts and crafts studio, where she holds workshops to make miniature food with polymer clay. The *noi yan cham mei* restaurant may now be shut, but it always holds a special place in the hearts of many locals for its "a bit Western, but not entirely so" delicious delights.

提到長洲節慶，很多人都會立即想起太平清醮，以及隨節日而生的平安包、搶包山和飄色巡遊等食物和活動。然而，長洲的傳統節慶不只得太平清醮。長洲有着深厚的歷史文化，不同祖籍的居民也把他們家鄉的信仰和習俗帶到長洲，其中天后誕和北帝誕也是島上盛事。

Speaking of Cheung Chau, many immediately think of the Bun Festival and related events such the bun tower climbing competition and the parade of deities called piu sik. Yet the famous Bun Festival is not the only traditional festival celebrated by islanders. The rich cultural heritage of Cheung Chau is found upon various ancestral religions and rituals. The Tin Hau Festival and the Pak Tai Festival are also seen as major events on the island.

Pak Tai Festival 3rd March (Lunar Calendar)

Pak Tai Festival

北帝
Pak Tai

On the far end of Pak She Street is the Yuk Hui Temple, which is also named Pak Tai Temple. Built in 1783, this magnificent temple is listed as a Grade I historical building by the Antiquities Advisory Committee.

When a pandemic broke out in 1777, fishermen travelled to Huiyang to carry a statue of Pak Tai back to Cheung Chau in the hope of suppressing the plague. Pak Tai, the god of water with power over the wind and the rain, has been hailed by generations of fishermen as the guardian of the sea. During the Pak Tai Festival, people bring tea, wine, fruits and vegetables to the temple. Community groups organise qilin dances and bring Pak Tai statues they worship at home to the temple to celebrate the deity's birthday. Large-scale Cantonese opera performances are staged at the basketball court outside the temple. Apart from the Pak Tai Festival, islanders carry out the Yau Long ritual at the Dragon Boat Festival to welcome Pak Tai onto their dragon boats for a ride.

The Pak Tai Temple of Cheung Chau houses also many historical artefacts. Yee Yuet, a Song Dynasty sword that was believed to have the power to ward off evil, was found missing in 1971. According to Kung Sheung Daily News, locals sought the whereabouts of the sword by drawing fortune sticks at the temple, with the oracle saying it would be recovered shortly. It finally took 46 days for the ancient sword to be found, after a habitual thief nicknamed "The Flying Spider" revealed its location during a police interrogation.

北帝誕

農曆三月初三

玉虛宮
Yuk Hui Temple

沿北社街走到尾，即可看到一座宏偉古雅的廟宇——玉虛宮，又稱北帝廟。這座古廟建於乾隆四十八年（1783年），有近二百四十年歷史，獲古物諮詢委員會評定為一級歷史建築物。相傳長洲於乾隆四十二年（1777年）疫症肆虐，因此漁民遠赴惠陽迎接北帝神像回島。北帝被視為水神，被認為能主宰風雨，被漁民奉為海上守護神。北帝誕期間，人們紛紛到廟內上香，及帶備齋菜、茶酒、鮮果等拜祭。島上社團亦會舞麒麟，帶同自己供奉的北帝到廟內賀誕，以及在廟前的籃球場辦大型神功戲。除了北帝誕外，島民在端午節亦有「遊龍」儀式，即恭請北帝到他們的龍船上「遊船河」，以祈求水陸安寧、魚蝦大順。

長洲北帝廟內有不少具歷史價值的文物，其中一把相信可以辟邪的宋代寶劍，曾一度被偷。根據1971年3月20日的工商日報，古劍二月被盜，當時居民求神問卜，簽文指古劍將會在短時間內尋回，果然，在古劍失蹤後四十六日，警方在觀塘截查外號「飛天蠄蟧」的慣竊賊時，他竟稱知道古劍下落，警方於是循他的口供搜索，終尋回古劍，成為一時新聞熱話。

遊船河
Dragon Boats

Tin Hau Festival 23rd March (Lunar Calendar)

Tin Hau Festival

The birthday of the goddess Tin Hau is of utmost significance to those who live by the sea. Tin Hau is believed to have the power to foretell the weather and can save fishermen from shipwrecks.

Known for its fishery industry, Cheung Chau has four Tin Hau temples. They are located at Sai Wan, Pak She (a temple inside an elderly care home), Tai Shek Hau, and Nam Tam. In the past, these temples were usually built along the coastline, but now most of them are found inland because of land reclamation. Among them, the one in Sai Wan is most frequented by worshipers and has the grandest Tin Hau Festival celebrations.

Tin Hau's birthday is 23 March in the Lunar calendar, but Sai Wan celebrates the festival on 18 March instead. Legend has it that the path to the temple was dark with no streetlamp, so the celebration was scheduled on an earlier date so that the moon would still be out to illuminate the way. Another saying is that in the old days, fishermen used bright lights to attract and catch fish at night. As 15 March is a full moon day, the sky would be too bright for the fishing lights. Seeing that it would be impossible for the fishermen to work, they chose to celebrate the Tin Hau Festival instead.

The celebration usually continues for a few days. Apart from the lion dance, dragon dance, and burning incense, a stage is built by the sea to present Cantonese opera performances in honour of the deity. Another ritual is to "compete for the firecracker". A special firecracker named "Pao Dam" was lit and shot into the sky, and those who managed to snatch it could use it in exchange for a Tin Hau statue. However, after the riots in 1967, the government announced a ban on firecrackers. As a result, people opted for shooting the Pao Dam with a slingshot instead in the 70s. It was later replaced by a lucky draw format in 1995.

比起太平清醮，不少水上人更重視天后誕。相傳天后自小有預測天氣的異能，能在海難時拯救漁民，因此長年與兇惡的大海共存的水上人都篤信天后娘娘能保平安，漁船上亦多有供奉天后。以漁業起家的長洲，足足有四座天后廟，分別位於西灣、北社（該廟位於老人院範圍內）、大石口和南氹。以往天后廟多建於海邊，現時位於較內陸位置的天后廟，都是後來填海之故，令其遠離海邊。但長洲仍有天后廟位於海旁，面朝大海，如西灣和南氹的天后廟，景色優美。當中以西灣天后廟香火最為鼎盛，天后誕的慶典也最隆重。

坊間的天后誕皆為農曆三月廿三，但西灣的天后誕卻提早幾日，定於三月十八日，相傳因為當年往返西灣天后廟進香之路缺乏街燈照明，大眾出入不方便，因此趁尚有月光的日子提早進行。亦有說指過去罟仔艇用大光燈捕魚，因十五月圓，月光過亮而照不到魚，不適合漁民作業，索性就選這日為誕日。一連幾日的慶典，除了舞獅、進香拜祭外，傳統上亦會在海邊搭建神功戲棚，往時海上總泊滿來看戲和參與盛會的漁船。此外亦有「搶花炮」儀式，花炮是綁有編號的爆竹，又稱「炮膽」，爆竹點燃後炮膽升天，成功搶奪「炮膽」，可以換取天后神像。但 1967 年暴動後，政府禁止點燃爆竹，於是由七十年代起改為用彈弓把「炮膽」彈上天讓善信搶奪，1995 年更改為抽花炮，氣氛大不如前。

天后誕

農曆三月廿三

Cheung Chau Bun Festival 8th April (Lunar Calendar)

Cheung Chau Bun Festival

Cheung Chau is packed with tourists every year during the Cheung Chau Bun Festival. Ping On buns, the Piu Sik parade and the bun scrambling competition have almost become the only things that represent the island.

The Cheung Chau Bun Festival, also known as "Tai Ping Qing Jiao" or "Da Jiao", originated from the events in 1777. Islanders travelled to Huizhou to carry the Pak Tai statue to Cheung Chau, hoping to invite the deity to suppress a pandemic. Since then, Da Jiao has continued annually for two centuries and has never once stopped even during the times of the Japanese occupation.

Da Jiao takes place over five days, in which a dozen rituals are carried out back-to-back. They include inviting and parading the gods, buddhābhiseka, starting the Jiao, staging Cantonese opera performances, and the bun tower climbing competition. Participants pray for luck and prosperity and commemorate the dead through these events.

For three days, people on Cheung Chau have to abstain from eating meat (McDonald's only sells vegetarian options too). In the past, local events were quite simple. But in the 60s, it started to turn into a carnival-like celebration with the bun tower climbing competition being the highlight, attracting many tourists to the island.

In the early days, there was more than one bun tower. Words such as "Peace" and "Prosperity" were stamped on the buns. These buns are believed to bring peace and protection to the people—so the more buns the better. The bun towers were thus built taller and taller and a snatching contest was initiated. This ultimately led to the bun tower collapse accident in 1978, injuring more than 100 people. The event was banned until 2005. By then, all words on the buns were changed to "Ping On", meaning peace to all. Tourism on Cheung Chau has since been reaching new heights.

Cheung Chau natives firmly believe that Da Jiao would affect the prosperity of the whole island. Hence all the rituals and events must hold to a certain standard. However in 1962, they broke the tradition of hiring Hok Lo Taoist priests and invited Chiuchow Taoist priests to carry out the rituals instead. In that year, Hong Kong was badly hit by Typhoon Wanda, causing many deaths and injuries and leaving some to speculate whether the two events were linked. From then onwards, only Hok Lo Taoist priests are hired for Da Jiao on Cheung Chau.

During the COVID-19 outbreak from 2020 to 2022, many events of the festival have massively been scaled down. The Piu Sik parade and bun tower climbing competition have also been cancelled. A festival that was born from a pandemic ultimately had to give way to another pandemic.

Reference materials:
"Journal of History and Culture: Commemorating the 200th Anniversary of the Founding of Cheung Chau" Cheung Chau Chinese Chamber of Commerce

農曆四月八

太平清醮

每年太平清醮期間，長洲都會擠得水泄不通，島外遊人蜂擁而至，平安包、飄色巡遊、搶包山幾乎成了長洲的代名詞。長洲太平清醮起源於上文提到的1777年瘟疫，當年居民遠赴惠州請北帝到長洲，及後每年打醮，至今有二百多年歷史，日治時期也未曾間斷。醮期為期五日，期間有迎神、開光、起醮、神功戲、走神、水祭、走船、搶包山等等十多個儀式密密進行，超渡亡者，為生者祈福。其中三日需守齋（長洲麥當勞亦會在這時期提供素包）。以往打醮為地區活動，較為簡單，自六十年代起漸漸成為帶有嘉年華色彩，吸引島外遊客慕名而至的大型盛事，當中最觸目的要數搶包山。早期包山不只一座，各個社團都會製作自己的包山，印上「北社」、「安」、「福」等字眼，相傳包子可保平安，愈多愈好，遂出現搶包山傳統，後來包山愈疊愈高，及至1978年發生包山倒塌意外，致多人受傷，逐被禁止。直到2005年包山重出江湖，但所有包子改為清一色「平安」二字，長洲旅遊業自此亦走上頂峰。

長洲人篤信打醮影響全島福祉，不容有失，惟1962年就打破了聘請鶴佬道士的慣例，改為聘請潮洲道士團，不幸地那年颶風溫黛襲港，死傷慘重，有人認為兩者有所關連，自此以後長洲打醮回復鶴佬道士。2020年至2022年，太平清醮因新冠肺炎及限聚令，大幅簡化，飄色和搶包山等環節均取消。因瘟疫而生的節慶，最終要給疫症讓路。

參考資料：
《長洲建墟市二百周年歷史及文化特刊》長洲華商會

Chapter 03

第三章

Legacy

兩代

都說香港是個大商場，在市區不論吃飲玩樂都離不開商場，店舖食肆清一色為大型連鎖店。反之，長洲仍然保留強烈街道文化，除了幾間大型連鎖超市和便利店外，街上小店和餐廳大都是自己生意，甚至不少是幾代經營的老字號，家人間的苦與甜、上一代的智慧、新一代的創意、與街坊的多年情誼，通通都緊繫店內。面對家族生意，一眾店主都有着打工仔所沒有的情義結和執著。

Hong Kong is often said to be one giant shopping mall, wherein shops and eateries are usually large chains.

Cheung Chau, on the other hand, has retained a strong street culture. Besides a few supermarkets and convenience stores, most shops and restaurants are independent businesses, with many being around for generations. Wisdom from ancestors, the creativity of the younger generations and the enduring bonds between neighbours have all opened a window into the bittersweet experiences of the family business.

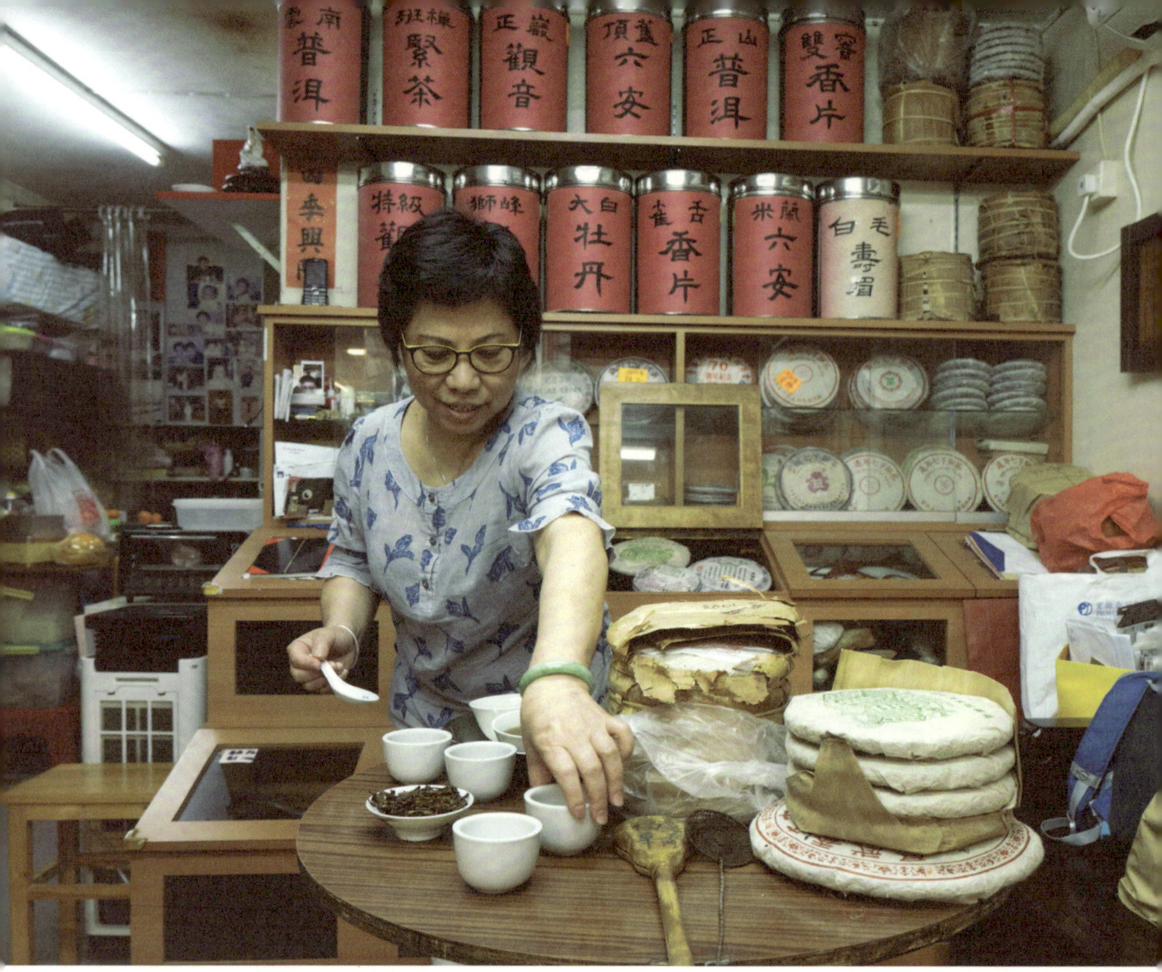
普洱
緊茶
正巖
觀音
六安
正山
普洱
雙窨
香片
特級
獅峰
大白
牡丹
雀舌
香片
六安
白毛
壽眉

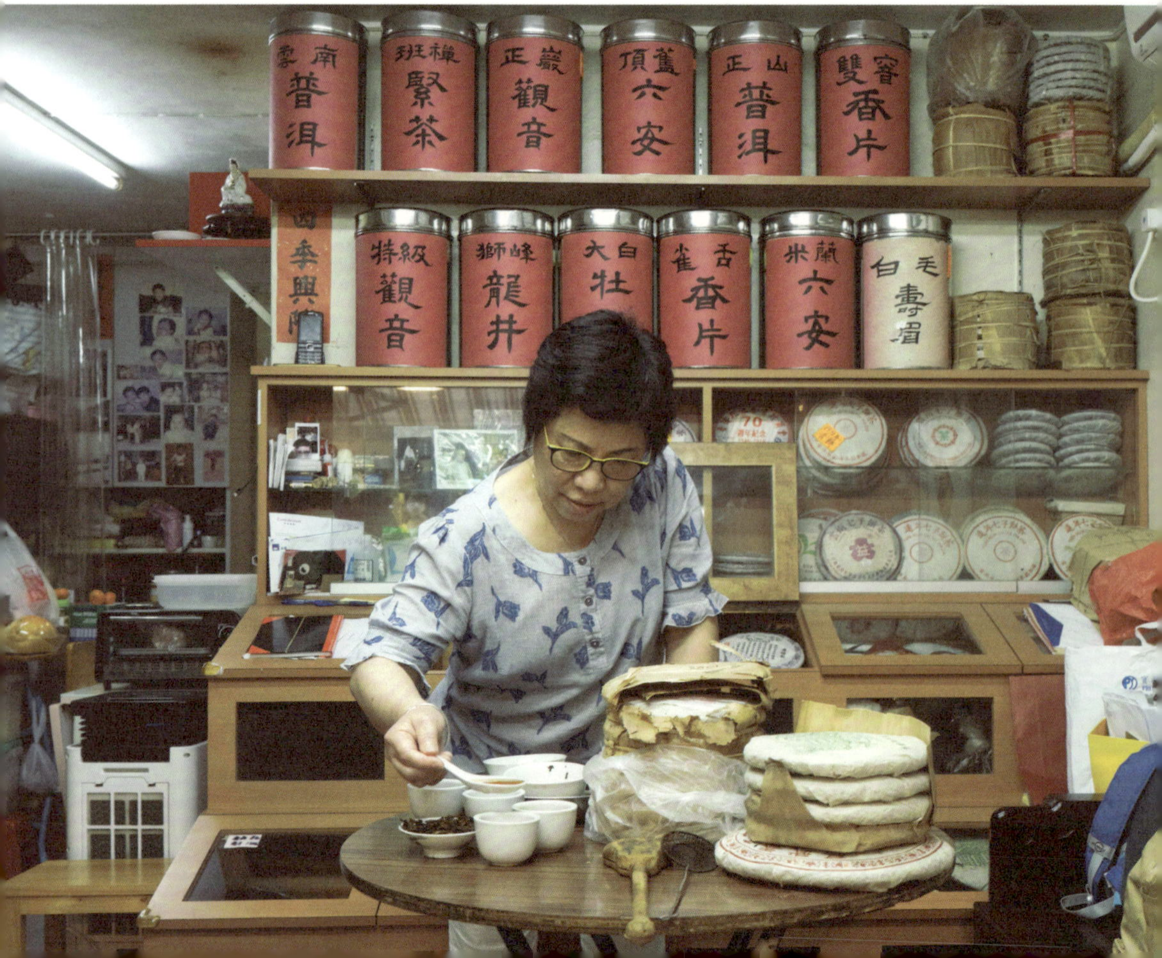
普洱
緊茶
正巖
觀音
六安
正山
普洱
雙窨
香片
特級
觀音
獅峰
龍井
大白
雀舌
香片
六安
白毛
壽眉

福華茶莊

Fook Wah Tea Co.

「熟茶之父」創福華茶莊
女承父業 毋忘初心

福華茶莊位於一個不大起眼的後街轉角，但創辦人盧鑄勳卻是茶業界內無人不曉的大師。他發明的熟茶發酵技術，大大縮短了青茶發酵轉化成紅茶的時間，故被尊稱為「熟茶之父」。盧師傅的長女黃太娓娓道來：「本來生茶變熟茶至少要三年，但經爸爸的加工處理，即蒸茶、焗倉，只需催熟半年便可飲用。」

黃太十三歲便開始掌店。「小時六兄弟姊妹都會幫手，但正式由我負責看舖該是 1974 年。那時長洲只有官校，連明愛[1]也未有，過幾年我妹妹才上第一屆女仔班。我讀完小學後派不到中學，自然就去舖頭幫手打點。」

盧鑄勳生於潮州，十歲時入學讀書，但翌年遇日本侵華輟學。1945 年 8 月，即日本宣佈無條件投降的兩星期後，乘船到澳門找機會。他經熟人介紹下到英記茶莊做雜工送貨，一年後調升到工場，學習篩焙和蒸製各類舊茶。

當年紅茶銷量和價格遠較青茶高，盧師傅見此靈機一動，着手研究如何把青茶發酵轉化成紅茶。他在青茶加水後用麻袋蓋着發酵，經數次反堆後轉紅至七八成乾，再放入貨倉焗。反覆試驗後，漸漸掌握到理想水量和溫度等訣竅。工場是盧師傅實踐抱負的重地，卻是黃太的兒時夢魘：「小時候我最怕要去倉，就像一個黑黷黷的大蒸爐，又翳熱又潮濕，還有很多曱甴四圍爬。每次要入去都如受罰般，但爸爸卻從無怨言。」

盧師傅不願一世替別人打工，便於 1954 年帶着獨門秘方來到香港，與友人在長洲創立福華號。茶莊的舊店位於新興街，就在屠場空地旁。盧師傅除出在佔地二三千呎的工場加工茶葉，還要穿梭星馬泰傾生意，而黃太的母親則在門口邊賣茶邊做手作幫補家計。

八零年北灣收地，茶莊被逼遷址，但屋漏偏逢連夜雨。「六七月要搬，但媽媽在三月打打下麻雀便突然走了。」媽媽的撒手人寰，令黃太放棄離開長洲外闖的念頭。「我本來都想出香港見識，雖在家中排行第三，但身為大女，總得留下照顧家人的開支。」黃太從當眼的玻璃櫃拿出一幀攝於 1953 年 6 月 7 日的照片，藍天白雲的背景下右方男子身穿深藍西裝，前左方女子燙了一頭斜瀏海波浪短髮。「這就是我爸爸和媽媽。」憶起亡母，黃太不住拭淚：「媽媽走得早，所以我們將他們的照片用電腦加工上色，成了他們的唯一合照。」

八十年代中，內地愈來愈少青茶運港，工場式微。盧氏一家生活漸見拮据，甚至要考慮借貸度日，盧師傅要隻身前往越南找茶葉，一去便是數年。「那是因為爸爸把自己的心血秘方告訴了大陸人，他們

[1]「長洲明愛聖保祿職業先修學校」創校於 1973 年，正值香港輕工業發達之時。1996 年改名為「明愛聖保祿職業先修中學」，後於 2001 年再改名為「明愛聖保祿中學」，終於 2007 年停辦。

拿來自己加工，用不着我們了。」黃太嘆一口氣：「很多行內人都話爸爸傻，但他是老實人，怎會藏私呢。不過我知爸爸沒有後悔，始終普洱熟茶得以發揚光大。」她邊說邊走到店後方的廚房，拿出兩套茶盅茶杯，又取煲燒水。「來，試試你便知道分別。生普是很香，但遠不如熟洱醇潤。」黃太對茶對人的熱情，一如先父。

盧師傅從不吝於傳授技術，新星茶莊的楊老莊主亦師承其下。新星茶莊為紀念熟茶的香港發明史，製作了一批用勐海地區的水發酵的熟茶餅，並以盧師傅命名。然而，徒弟的心意終究不是自家品牌，令他始有缺失。黃太深知年邁的父親念念不忘，便跟兄弟商量，找來一批上好茶葉製作茶餅，印上「福華號宋聘唛」的名號，作為這位茶藝大師的九十歲大壽的賀禮。

1999 年，茶莊第三度遷店，亦即大新後街近昇昌里交界的現址。黃太說：「上手賣衫仔，而我始終唔想唔賣茶，就邊賣童裝邊賣茶，又在店湊仔煮飯。」即使生意一直萎縮，黃太仍處之泰然：「現在有少少收入、有瓦遮頭、有飯開，街坊經過又可以傾兩句，都夠啦。」現在的福華號除了坐地茶櫃，還有一張立着各式毛公仔的沙發。店與街，只隔一道如包書膠般薄的透明屏障，不時見到圍着圍裙的黃太，親切地招呼生客熟客。

Fook Wah Tea Co.: **SHOULDERING THE LEGACY OF PU'ER TEA GODFATHER**

Fook Wah Tea Co. might be a small shop tucked in a backstreet corner, but its founder Lu Zhuxun is a renowned master and a game changer of the tea industry. The fermentation technique he invented has drastically shortened the time needed to turn raw tea into ripe tea, earning him the title “Godfather of Ripe Pu‘er Tea”.

His eldest daughter Mrs. Wong explains: “It used to take at least three years to ripen raw tea. But with my father‘s processing method, which involves steaming and baking, it takes only half a year before it is consumable.”

Mrs. Wong has been managing the store since she was 13. “When we were little, all six siblings had to help out,” she says. “But I only took over officially in 1974. At that time, Cheung Chau only had one government school. Caritas had yet to be established1, my younger sister only joined its first girls‘ class several years later. I wasn’t admitted to any secondary school after primary school, so naturally I returned to the tea shop and helped out.”

Born in Chiuchow, Lu Zhuxun started school at the age of ten, but had to drop out when Japan began its invasion the year after. In August 1945—two weeks after Japan had announced its unconditional surrender, Mr. Lu travelled to Macau by boat to look for opportunities. Through referral he found employment at Ying Kee Tea House. He was assigned to the workshop after one year of performing chores and deliveries, learning how to refine, roast, and steam all types of aged teas.

1 Caritas St. Paul Prevocational School was established in 1973 when the light industry was at its prime in Hong Kong. It was renamed as Caritas St. Paul Secondary School in 2001, before ceasing operation in 2007.

觀音

龍井
正山
普洱
普洱
香片
香片
觀音
六安

Back in those days, the sales volume and price of red tea were much higher than those of green tea. Mr. Lu had a flash of inspiration and began to research how green tea could be fermented into red tea. He tried dampening the green tea, then covered them with burlap sacks for fermentation. After turning the tea piles several times, the leaves would turn red and be left to air dry until they were 70-80% dry, before being transferred to the storage for roasting. After rounds of experiments, Mr. Lu found the ideal formula, such as the best water ratio and temperature.

Mr. Lu did not want to work under someone else for the rest of his life, so he brought his secret formula to Hong Kong and established Fook Wah Tea Co. with some friends in Cheung Chau in 1954.

The old shop was located on San Hing Street, next to the empty grounds of a slaughterhouse. Apart from overseeing the tea processing in the 2,000- to 3,000-feet workshop, Mr. Lu also frequented Singapore, Malaysia, and Thailand for business dealings, whereas Mrs. Lu would manage the shop and sell some handicrafts on the side for extra income.

The workshop where Mr. Lu set and achieved his ambitions was a terrifying place for the young Mrs. Wong. "I was really afraid of visiting the storage when I was little," she recalls. "It felt like being inside of a massive steam oven: dark, stuffy and humid, with cockroaches crawling around. It felt like a punishment being in there each time, but my father never had a word of complaint."

In 1980, Fook Wah was forced to move as the government was reclaiming lands around the north bay. And as the saying goes, it never rains but it pours. "We had to move between June and July, but my mother suddenly passed away when she was in the middle of a mahjong game in March."

Faced with her mother's sudden death, Mrs. Wong gave up the idea of venturing out of Cheung Chau. "I had thought of exploring Hong Kong. While I am the third-born in the family, I am the eldest daughter, so I had to stay behind to take care of the family and its expenses."

Mrs. Wong takes out a photo dated 7 June 1953 from a glazed cabinet in the centre of the shop. Under the blue skies stood a man in a dark blue suit and, on his right, a woman in short hair with a wavy fringe. "These are my father and mother." Tears stream down her face as Mrs. Wong remembers her mother: "My mother left too early. So we photoshop-ed and colourised this picture, which is their only photo together."

As less and less green tea was being exported to Hong Kong from Mainland China in the 80s, the workshop's business gradually declined. The Lu family was soon rocked by financial challenges and, at some point, even had to consider loans to make ends meet. Set off to source tea leaves in Vietnam, Mr. Lu was gone for several years. "That all happened because my father shared his precious formula with people from Mainland China. They could process the tea leaves on their own and no longer needed us."

Mrs. Wong sighs and continues: "Many folks in the trade said my father was foolish. But he was an honest man, so how could he have kept anything just for himself? But I know my father never regretted [the decision], as ripe pu'er tea has since been popularised and flourished."

雲南普洱
班禪緊茶
正巖觀音
六安
正山普洱
雙窨香片
四季興隆
特級觀音
獅峰龍井
大白牡丹
雀舌
米蘭六安
白毛壽眉

She takes out two tea sets from the kitchen at the back of the shop, and puts some water to boil. "Come on, have a taste and you will know the difference. Raw pu'er is fragrant, but is far less mellow and luscious than ripe pu'er." Mrs. Wong is as passionate about tea and people as her late father.

Mr. Lu was always eager to share his knowledge and skills with others, and Mr. Kings Yeung, the founder of the established chain Sun Sing Tea, was one of his apprentices. To commemorate the important role that Hong Kong had played in the invention of ripe pu'er, Sun Sing made a batch of tea cakes named after Mr. Lu.

Despite a gesture as kind as that, Mr. Lu was still overwhelmed by a sense of loss because the product was not sold under the Fook Wah brand. Mrs. Wong and her brothers thus produced a batch of premium tea cakes, stamped with the brand "Fook Wah Song Ping" ("Song Ping" references an extremely rare, vintage pu'er tea brand), as a gift for the tea master's 90th birthday.

In 1999, Fook Wah had to relocate for the third time to its current site at the intersection of Tai San Back Street and Shing Cheong Lane. "The last tenant sold clothing and I did not want to stop selling tea," Mrs. Wong says. "That's why I have come to selling both kid's wear and tea, while also taking care of the little ones and cooking meals here."

Though business has been dwindling, Mrs. Wong remains unruffled: "Now that I can have some sort of income, a roof over my head, food to eat, and neighbours to catch up with whenever they pass by, that's good enough."

百年泉安鳳翔紙號

Chuen On Fung Cheung Papercraft

百年泉安鳳翔紙號
幾代人的生死教育

俊文的紮作祖業已有過百年歷史。爺爺的婆婆早已擺街檔售賣衣紙香燭，後來爺爺正式立店，取名「泉安」，而爸爸接手後再添上自己的名字，現在街坊熟客多簡稱紙號為「鳳翔」。

俊文的爺爺是喃嘸師傅，衣紙紮作之外，還精通雕刻、看風水、擇吉日、計算時辰八字。「很多人都只會識一兩樣，但爺爺非常好學，會特意請不同專長的師傅返來幫手，順便偷師。」俊文提起爺爺時總是充滿欽佩。

按照水上人傳統，紅事白事要分開處理，任何交疊均被視作不吉利。「他們覺得污糟咗，就返唔到轉頭。」俊文的爺爺認為白事是「眼淚錢」，故堅持只做紅事。除了保佑新人、「脫褐」[1] 儀式和其他嫁娶習俗，還會主持新船下水禮、替廟宇神像開光、請祖先上神枱等。

太平清醮亦是紙號的年度大事。相傳清朝中葉瘟疫肆虐，長洲人便於北帝廟附近設壇拜祭祈福，期間齋戒積德，漸漸演變成世代相傳的民俗。除了做法事和布置醮場，紙號亦準備塔香予信眾買來祈福，又會進口足足有一個成年人那麼粗、至少要三四天才能燃盡的柱香，矗立醮場前點燃。紙號亦曾兼營香燭批發，廠房設在新界北，專門供貨予連鎖超市。不過後來因為上架費日漲，加上久久才結帳一次，最終結業收場。

家族生意世代相傳，俊文自小便要邊學邊做，旺季時更是忙過不停。「以前要兼顧紮作，一放學就要回店幫手，長假期都沒得去玩，因總會遇上大時大節，如復活節便和天后誕撞期，一家人要齊齊做到凌晨一點才開飯。」

紙號二十年多前遷到熙來攘往的大新海傍道、街市對面的現址。門前掛滿紮作，沒有招牌，但總不乏街坊購物聊天。現在店內大部分紮作也是跟中國內地來貨，但俊文每年盂蘭節仍會按照傳統，親自製作一首闊近兩米、高約一米半的郵輪，祭給 1971 年颱風露絲襲港時、在大嶼山東北角對出遇難的八十八位佛山號船員。

俊文的爺爺生前從不沾手白事，而爸爸也是得知島上有孤兒寡婦未能負擔喪葬，才出手幫忙。俊文說：「爸爸的性格是幫人幫到盡。他常說，每次幫手都要當係自己死老豆咁着緊，每一個細節都要跟足。」但兩父子從沒忘記爺爺要紅白二事分開的叮囑，遂在紅磡另外設店，專門處理殯儀服務。

爺爺是喃嘸師傅，而自己的日常工作亦需協助執行各宗教儀式，但俊文強調自己是無神論者。他引用儒家的哲學：未能事人，焉能事鬼。「水上人特別迷信，有些明明是普通傷風感冒，但覺得『周身唔聚財』(渾身不自在)，以為找我們望望再拜神就沒事。這些我都會和他們傾，再勸他們去看醫生。」他指出，後事涉及一系列煩瑣程序，加上家屬在失去摯親後難免情緒波動，因此更需要適度抽離、保持冷靜，才能最有效幫助客人過渡難關。

俊文視對死者的尊重和安撫在生者為日常工作的首要任務。殯儀形式再不同，他也會慎重地打點逝者的最後一里路。他說：「幫先人，真係幫到人㗎。」初回店幫忙打點時，有位朋友同時失去雙親，而他家境清寒，對喪事更是徬徨無助。俊文的爸爸得知後二話不說，提出按成本價再打七折。「當時我愕了然，本來只想問可不可以略減兩三千，沒想過要家人做蝕本生意，但爸爸很理所當然地覺得有能力就要幫。」除了巧手工藝，以及對人的尊重，紙號亦承載着三代人的慈心。

而除了殯儀的實際事務，俊文也會兼任心理輔導員。相較久病離世，毫無預警的死亡常常令在生的至親多了一份內疚，自責未能及早看出端倪，這些俊文都會特別細心聆聽。「曾有位客人因太太在夢中猝逝不住自責，認為自己要是在半夜去廁所時察覺的話，或能及時救治。其實正常都不會無端端拍醒身邊人查看啦，但傷痛時很易會鑽牛角尖。呢啲都要慢慢疏導。」

[1]「脫褐」又稱「脫學」，是新郎新娘過渡至成人階段的儀式，屬水上人婚禮中一項重要儀節。

相較靈異見聞，俊文認為塵世的恩仇情愁更峰迴路轉，而從事殯儀業，更是見盡世情百態。除了爭產不和、名分爭執而在靈堂大打出手等較戲劇化的場境，當家屬持不同信仰或對儀式的意見相左時，俊文也會幫忙調解。

「我常說，殯儀是硬件，重點還是人。」即使工作時間很長，店舖營業朝八晚七，代辦殯儀時更是朝八晚十一，但他始終視之為終生事業。「做得呢行，咩時間都會收到電話。如前幾日才有朋友凌晨兩點來電，說他爸爸走了，問要如何處理。總之幾點我都會應機，最緊要幫到人。」

俊文的爺爺數年前以九十多高齡離世。他因重症臥床於市區醫院，依賴強心針續命，等待親人回港見最後一面。「我知姑姐抵港見過後就不會再打針，然後就只剩幾個鐘，但碰巧那天有場殯儀，爸爸或我，總有一人要留在長洲打點。」結果俊文選擇留島處理公事。自言眼淺的他語帶感觸：「就算我清楚知道爺爺幾時走，但始終送唔到佢最後一程，所以人真的要趁在生時珍惜。」

長洲變遷的速度有目共睹，但殯儀關乎對先人、傳統的尊重，較少外來因素影響。這些年來，小變化總會有，如以往會將遺體從長洲醫院運到海濱亭化妝入殮，但因人來人往不太方便而取消；通宵打齋、招魂等或會滋擾鄰近民居的儀式亦不復再。「不過大體上，我們始終想跟足舊時的禮數。例如打齋，出面打三四小時就完。而我們多數四點打到十點，有些水上人甚至要打幾場才行。」

時至今日，工作量遠不如往日吃重，但俊文也會請六歲兒子在空閒時幫忙，負責排櫈派水等簡單工作。「我只當是生死教育，順便可以見見街坊。至於往後他會否繼承，全然是他的選擇。」

Chuen On Fung Cheung Papercraft: **LIFE AND DEATH EDUCATION AT THE CENTURY-OLD WORKSHOP**

Nick's family business, Chuen On Fung Cheung Papercraft, has a remarkable history of over 100 years, dating back to the grandmother of Nick's grandfather who first sold papier-mâché offerings, incense sticks and candles on the streets. His grandfather later opened a brick-and-mortar shop and named it "Chuen On". After Nick's father took over the shop, he added his name "Fung Cheung" and now locals usually refer to the shop as "Fung Cheung".

Nick's grandfather was a Taoist priest. Apart from paper crafting, he was also an expert in carving, feng-shui, auspicious day picking, and BaZi reading—a Chinese astrological method to foretell destiny based on one's date and time of birth. "Most people only knew one or two of these trades, but my grandfather was a keen learner. He would invite practitioners of different expertise to help out at the shop so that he could learn from them on the side." Nick always speaks of his grandfather with admiration.

Boat dwellers—a majority of Cheung Chau's population—used to (and some still do) insist that red affairs (celebratory rituals) and white affairs (funeral rites) must be handled separately, and any overlap between the two would be regarded as ominous. "They believe that once it's 'tainted', there's no going back," says Nick. His grandfather, who regarded white affairs as a "business of tears", only handled red affairs. Besides the "Rite of Passage" [1] ritual that protects newlyweds and other marital customs, his grandfather would also host other ceremonies, including new ship launching

1 The "Rite of Passage" is an important component of the wedding ceremony of the boat dwellers. It symbolises the readiness of the bride and groom to form their own family.

粒
品

ceremonies and the rituals of enlightening the deity images at temples and inviting ancestors to the altar.

The Cheung Chau Bun Festival is a huge annual event for the shop. During the Qing Dynasty, a plague raged over Cheung Chau, so locals set up an altar near the Pak Tai Temple to worship and pray for blessings. They also abstained from eating meat for three days, which gradually became a folk custom being passed from generation to generation. Apart from performing the rituals and decorating the ritual site, the shop also prepares spiral incense for worshipers to purchase. Nick also imports and places giant incense sticks that can burn for three to four days in front of the site.

Fung Cheung used to run a joss stick wholesale business alongside, with a factory in the northern New Territories to supply supermarket chains. However the wholesale operation eventually went out of business due to spiking slotting fees and lengthy payment schedules.

Now taking the helm of the family business, Nick learned by doing from a young age. “I had to help hand-make paper offerings back then, so I came back to the shop immediately after school,” he recalls. “Work was busy during long holidays as well, because they always coincided with festivities or major events, like the Easter holidays occurred at the same time as the Tin Hau Festival. It was all hands on deck and the whole family would not have time for dinner until 1 a.m.”

The shop moved to its current location opposite the wet market on the busy Tai San Praya Road two decades ago. Though without a shop sign, the storefront is lined with papier-mâché offerings and there are always locals shopping or stopping by for just a chat.

Most of the products at the shop are now imported from Mainland China, but Nick still follows his father's practice and makes an exception every year during the Ghost Festival. He always makes from scratch a 2-metre-wide, 1.5-metre-tall paper cruise, as an offering for the 88 crew members who had died in the SS Fatshan shipwreck near Lantau Island when Typhoon Rose hit Hong Kong in 1971.

Nick's grandfather never provided services for funerals when he was alive, and Nick's father only started this service when he learned of orphans and widows who could not afford the funeral fees on the island. Nick says: "My father is the kind of person who wants to help as much as he can. As he always says, we have to be as conscientious as we can for every service, as if it's the funeral of our father. We need to make sure that every detail is handled properly." The two never forget grandpa's reminder to separate red and white affairs, so they set up another shop in Hung Hom specifically for funeral services.

Nick stresses that he is an atheist, even though his daily work involves all kinds of religious ceremonies and his grandfather was a Taoist priest. He cites the Confucius saying: "You are not yet able to serve people—how can you serve ghosts and spirits? "

"Boat dwellers tend to be more superstitious. Some of them may feel very uneasy and think that everything would be fine after consulting us and saying some prayers—even though they only catch a cold. For cases like these, I would talk to them and persuade them to visit a doctor."

Funeral events often involve a series of trivial yet complicated procedures, not to mention handling the overwhelming emotions of clients who have just lost their loved ones. It is important, he notes, to remain calm and keep a certain emotional distance in order to provide the most effective help for clients in their difficult times.

Nick sees respecting the dead and comforting the living to be the most important tasks of his job. No matter how different the formats are, he always takes conscientious care of the final journey. "By helping the deceased, we also help the living." When he first returned to help out at the shop, a friend lost both his parents at the same time and struggled to pay for their funerals. After learning about his story, Nick's father offered a 30% discount on the cost without a second thought. "I was shocked. Initially I just wanted to ask whether we could knock some dollars off the price, I never expected my family to make an unprofitable deal. But my father thought it was only right to help as much as we could." Besides their delicate craftsmanship and respect for humanity, the shop also embodies the kindness of three generations.

Nick serves as a counsellor sometimes too. Unlike deaths by chronic illnesses, sudden passings often sadden families and friends with guilt, as they tend to blame themselves for not being able to spot the cues earlier. Nick thus pays closer attention to these cases. "There was one client whose wife passed away suddenly in her sleep. He blamed himself for not having noticed her situation when he went to the bathroom in the middle of the night. He thought she might have been able to receive medical help in time if he did," Neck says. "In reality, we seldom wake our partners up just to check on them, but it is easy to overthink when one is in grief. It takes time to release these emotions."

Compared to supernatural encounters, Nick believes that the enmity and conflicts between the living are much more haunting. Apart from disputes over inheritance that sometimes result in physical fights in the funeral hall, Nick would step in and mediate when family members argue over different religious traditions or rituals.

The shop of Fung Cheung operates from 8 a.m. to 7 p.m. and the team works from 8 a.m. to 11 p.m. on funeral days. Though the working hours are very long, he still sees it as his lifelong career.

"As I always say, the funeral is only a hardware, what matters the most are the people." Nick adds, "When you are in this business, you receive phone calls at any hour of the day. Like a friend called me at 2 a.m. several days ago. He said that his father had passed away and asked me what to do. I always answer phone calls no matter what time it is. What's important is to help people when they need it."

Nick's grandfather passed away a few years ago in his 90s. Bedridden at a hospital in the city, he lived on cardiotonic injections to buy time for family members abroad to fly back and meet him for the last time. "I knew that they would stop administering the shots after he saw my aunt. After that it would only be a matter of hours." Nick, who describes himself as someone who tears up easily, recalls in a cracking voice. "However, there was a funeral on that day, meaning either my father or I would have to stay on Cheung Chau to take care of it." In the end, Nick decided to stay for business. "Even though I knew exactly when my grandfather was going to go, I still could not be by his side when the time came. We need to appreciate the time we have with others while we can."

The speed of change on Cheung Chau has been obvious to all, but funeral practices are less affected as they represent the respect for ancestors and traditions. That said, there have been minor changes over the years. For example, the old practice of transporting the bodies from the Cheung Chau hospital to the Hoi Bun Pavilion for make-up and encoffining was cancelled due to its location on a crowded street; overnight ceremonies no longer take place to minimise disturbances to nearby residents. "But overall, we still want to follow the traditional customs as closely as possible. For example, funeral rituals in the city only last for three to four hours, but we usually perform them from 4 p.m. to 10 p.m. here. Some boat dwellers even ask for several rounds."

The workload nowadays is far less than before, but Nick still asks his six-year-old son to help out with simple tasks such as lining up stools and distributing bottled water when he is free. "I just see this as life and death education and a chance for him to meet the locals," says Nick. "As to whether he would inherit the business, I would leave the decision completely up to him."

興記士多

Hing Kee Beach Store

興記士多
長子的堅持

恐怕是受青春時代的當紅日劇《Beach Boys》影響，跟我一樣的八十後，或多或少都嚮往過這麼一種生活：搬到一個遠離煩囂的寧靜小島，開間海邊士多，平日賣賣汽水啤酒，隨時隨地撲進大海暢泳，晚上跟朋友把酒相聚，日日如是，沒有比這更寫意的人生了。位於長洲觀音灣的興記士多，在我眼中就像《Beach Boys》的化身，店主Derek曬得一身古銅，每次見到他，要不是在士多打點、與愛犬玩耍，就是在海上某隻風帆上乘風破浪。但一如日劇中的各人，在青春浪漫底下，其實各自帶着故事和失落，興記士多經歷的，也不盡是風和日麗。這間小小的海邊士多，接受過大自然的嚴峻試練，它盛載的是幾代人的心血，也是一個長子對這家族心血的承擔。

與興記士多的第三代主理人Derek相約在一個十二月的平日下午，時值冬天，沙灘只有小貓三兩，士多亦只有他和另一熟客，但他指：「我就係唔想咁旺，隱世一點，留給真正想來享受寧靜的人。」興記士多位於觀音灣，很多遊人在旁邊的長洲最大沙灘東灣便止步，令觀音灣相對清靜，而且明顯較多外國人，Derek指，以往很多修士和外國人居住長洲，觀音灣成了他們的後花園，又叫為(Afternoon Beach)。

興記士多由Derek的祖父開設，已有七十多年歷史，當時士多只是一間小屋，規模細小，賣些簡單的飲品，甚至連名號都欠奉。後來傳到Derek父親之手，改名為興記。Derek回憶起父親說：「他很勸力。他是家中長子，有六個弟妹，以前家裡很窮，阿爺在他廿幾歲時過身，阿爸獨力湊大六弟妹。」以前士多生意不夠糊口，夏天開檔，冬天就在山頭的農地種菜。由於客人多為外國人，父親收舖後還會到夜校學英文。

Derek也是家中長子，自小在長洲大，與海為伴，興記士多和觀音灣是他成長的一部分，直到中學他出香港讀書，及後在香港服裝行業工作了十幾年。他2009年結婚，翌年誕下兒子，再過四年誕下女兒，一切看似平順。但同一時間，父親身體漸漸變差，於是他於2013年決定回到長洲接手士多，那年他三十有七，而父親在兩年後離世，「好像是上天安排我這個時候回來接手一樣。」

跟父親共事的兩年，Derek 指難免多磨擦，譬如父親會覺得兒子維修硬件時要戴手套，「姐手姐腳」。他直言爸爸好嚴，因此他想為士多帶來新鮮事時，都是逐少逐少試探爸爸的底線，譬如以前士多只賣藍妹、嘉士伯啤酒，後來漸漸引進其他特色啤酒，包括本地手工啤，「阿媽會幫口說：『俾佢試吓啦！』見阿爸無鬧，就當他默認。」又例如，以前的屋仔是灰色鐵皮屋，後來油成亮眼有生氣的紅黃藍，又有更多水上活動設施供人租用，他更會大方地免費租場給朋友搞活動，如現場 DJ 打碟音樂派對，愈做愈有規模。周末遊人眾多，不時都見到父親的弟妹一起幫手看檔，甚為熱鬧，只可惜，父親已無緣見證和陪伴興記的成長。

雲淡風輕時，大海可愛可親，但遇上狂風暴雨，大海可把一切吞噬，包括一個人的意志。2017 及 2018 年，香港連續兩年經歷兩個超強颱風天鴿和山竹，風後整個香港滿目瘡痍，加上天文大潮，長洲受災嚴重，東堤的行人路幾乎全毀，Derek 記得山竹翌日回到興記，熟悉的屋仔被沙吞沒，親手鋪的英泥地全被吹爛，店內的牆穿了大洞，所有電器要報銷，「我見到簡直是震驚，即時大哭，那是爸爸和幾代人的心血。」他坦言，面對此情景，他有想過放棄，幸得媽媽勸他堅持，這次不幸，也體現了何謂一方有難，百方幫忙，不少興記的熟客、朋友都落手落腳幫忙剷沙，有外國客人甚至不上班、取消會議來幫忙，「因為大家都好愛這個沙灘，如果沙灘沒有了，可以去邊？」士多重開後，亦會有人用幾百元買啤酒，當是補助士多。這是大家的沙灘，大家的興記士多。

每逢冬天人流減少，Derek 就忙於維修士多，最近，興記在燒烤位置多了一道色彩豐富的矮欄，地上鋪了人工草皮，新增了吧檯等等，迎接更多喜歡這沙灘的人。不變的是，天氣好的日子，他還是會不顧一切跳進水裡，或揚起他的風帆乘風破浪，「如果唔鍾意海，我唔會堅持到咁耐。」

興記
TODAY SPECIAL
1. FISH & CHIPS $80
炸魚薯條
2. PORK CHOP SALAD
香煎豬扒沙律 $88
3. BEEF CRISPY BUN
香脆牛肉包 $42
COLD DRINK
4. HING KEE's SPECIAL
薄荷特飲 $38
5. RIBENA LEMON SODA
檸檬利賓納梳打 $32
TAKE AWAY
YOUR OWN TRASH
自己垃圾
自己清走
香港人加油

士　多
Gone SaiLing
興記
Coca-Cola
Coca-Cola
請勿攜帶外來食品／飲品
於本範圍享用
PLEASE DON'T BRING
OUTSIDE FOODS/
DRINKS IN THE AREA
Tip Box
PROTECT THE NATURE
保護大自然
=
PROTECT YOUR CHILDREN
保護你的小孩

Hing Kee Beach Store: **RIDING THROUGH THE STORMS**

Perhaps because of the popular Japanese TV drama *Beach Boys*, those who were born after the 80s have more or less fantasised a kind of life like this every day—move to a quiet island far away from the bustling city, open a seaside store for soda and beer, jump into the ocean for a swim whenever feel like it.

Hing Kee Beach Store located on Kwun Yam Wan looks like it came out of *Beach Boys*. Derek, the store's third-generation owner, is always found either managing the store, playing with his dog, or sailing on the sea.

But what Hing Kee Beach Store has experienced is not all sunshine and beauty. Having withstood the most rigorous tests from nature, this tiny beach store embodies the hard work of several generations, as well as the responsibilities now shouldered by Derek, the eldest son.

On a December weekday afternoon, there are just a handful of people on the beach besides Derek and another regular. "I don't want it to be too popular," says the suntanned owner. "I would rather it stays low-profile, so it can be for those who want to enjoy a bit of peace and tranquility." While many tourists stop at the nearby Tung Wan—Cheung Chau's biggest beach, Kwun Yam Wan was a quieter spot frequented by friars and expats, hence earning its nickname "The Afternoon Beach".

Hing Kee Beach Store was launched by Derek's grandfather more than 70 years ago. At that time, the store was only a small pavilion selling a limited selection of drinks. The store didn't even have a name until Derek's father took over. "My dad was very hardworking. He was the eldest of the six siblings," Derek says.

"The family was poor, and my grandad died when my dad was about 20 years old, so he had to raise his siblings all by himself." The income from the store alone was not sufficient for their livelihood, so his father ran the store in the summer and grew vegetables in a nearby farm in the winter. Since most of the customers were foreigners, his father went to a night school for English classes after closing the shop every day.

Derek, also the eldest son in the family, grew up on Cheung Chau with the sea keeping him company. Hing Kee Beach Store and Kwun Yam Wan played a huge part in his childhood until he moved to the city for secondary school and then worked in the clothing industry for more than ten years. He got married in 2009 and had a son the next year. His daughter was born four years later.

But just when everything seemed to be going well, his father's health deteriorated, so he returned to Cheung Chau to take the helm in 2013 when he was 37. His father passed away two years later. "It was as if fate had arranged for me to come back and take over at that time."

Quarrels were inevitable between the father and the son during the first two years of Derek's return. As his father was quite stubborn, he always had to take one step at a time to test the waters whenever he wanted to bring new ideas to the store. For instance, the store used to sell only Blue Girl and Carlsberg, but later introduced other specialty beers including locally crafted ones. "My mother would always help and say, 'Just let him try!' I took my father's silence as a green light."

Originally made of grey metal sheets, the store was later repainted with bright red, yellow and blue and stocked with more watersports essentials for rent. He would also generously lend the space to his friends for free to host events, such as live music parties with DJs. The store has slowly grown in scale over the years. His father's siblings often come to help during the weekends when there are more tourists. It is unfortunate that Derek's father can no longer witness and be part of Hing Kee's lively growth.

When the weather is calm, the sea is lovely; but when there is a storm, the sea can destroy everything, including one's will. In 2017 and 2018, Hong Kong experienced two super typhoons Hato and Mangkhut, after which the whole city was left desolated. Cheung Chau recorded severe damages, and the sidewalk along Cheung Chau Beach Road was almost eradicated entirely. Derek still remembers that shocking sight when he returned to Hing Kee the day after Typhoon Mangkhut—the familiar pavilion was subsumed by sand and the concrete floor he paved was completely destroyed. There was a giant hole in the wall inside the store, and all the electrical appliances were broken. "I was so shocked that I immediately burst into tears. That was my father's and several generations' hard work." He thought of giving up, but his mother encouraged him to keep going.

The silver lining of this misfortune was the overpouring support from their customers and friends. Many regulars came to help remove the sand from the store, some expats even took a day off and cancelled their meetings in order to help. "It is because everybody loves this beach. If the beach is gone, where can we go?" When the store reopened, some people paid several hundred dollars for just a couple of beers in a show of support. This is everyone's beach, and this is everyone's Hing Kee.

Though the store sees fewer visitors every winter, Derek is occupied with repairing and touching up. Some recent additions include a new colourful garden fence near the shop's barbeque area, artificial grass on the floor and a new bar table to welcome more visitors who share a love for this beach.

What remains unchanged is that on days of good weather, Derek would still hop into the water without a second thought or hoist a sail to ride the waves. "If I didn't like the ocean, I would not have lasted this long."

長洲花會

長洲花舍 Cheung Chau Garden

長洲花舍
當這花店沒有花

百足多爪的蕭爸爸是一個不折不扣的生意人，他曾在長洲經營肉檔和酒樓，更是長洲第一間花店「長洲花舍」的創辦人。

女兒 Betty 出生後，蕭爸爸覺得有需要另闢收入來源，翌年「長洲花舍」開業。蕭爸爸娓娓道來：「你知道為何我一個豬肉佬會貿然轉行賣花嗎？不就是因為當時這兒未有人賣呀。」島上首間花店，背後沒有任何浪漫因由，只是見機而作。曾涉足八個行業的蕭爸爸如數家珍：「我賣過豬肉、牛肉、燒臘、電器、水果，又曾過養魚，現在就經營酒樓和這花店。」

花店至今屹立三十多年，肉檔和酒樓的生意早上軌道，不過原來他也曾吃盡苦頭。「梅窩電器店開幕不夠兩個月便倒閉收場，結果賠了二十七萬。當時又適逢新街市落成，肉檔搬遷所需的裝修和競投費用，一時周轉不靈，我又不想開口借錢，唯有每天去粉麵檔吃兩碗淨麵填肚便算。」此後，蕭爸爸的投資作風亦轉趨保守，崇尚未雨綢繆。

「這場肺炎便證明我是對的，即使飲食業首當其衝，酒樓至今尚算穩健。」

三十多年前，這間島上首間花店開業，只有一位不諳花藝的員工坐鎮，接下訂單後，才預約師傅帶同鮮花乘船入長洲，即場完成製作便離開。耳濡目染下，那位員工和蕭爸爸漸漸掌握了基本技巧，才開始售賣花束。

2015 年農曆新年假後啟市那天，唯一的老員工突因要照顧孫兒而請辭。蕭爸爸一時間找不到人頂替，打算關門大吉，但女兒 Betty 不想父親多年心血白流，毅然接手花店。

十三歲便赴英升學的Betty坦言，經歷過不少掙扎後，才決定扛起擔子。「我本來計劃繼續升讀碩士，但媽媽病重，便匆匆完成學士學位回港陪伴。」兩年後媽媽離世，Betty從事市場推廣的全職一年，還是想回學府深造，繼續研究食物科學。就在那時，花舍的命運來到了分岔口，她便一邊修讀碩士，一邊打理花舍。

接棒後，Betty駭然發現花舍長年虧蝕。「鮮花捱上三兩日便變殘花，無人問津下，丟棄的花比賣出的還要多。」有見花舍八至九成的生意來自預購訂單，她便把心一橫，回到沒有存花的年代，待接下單才訂貨。「總不能因要門面光鮮而見蝕不止。」

大幅革新卻引起花舍結業的流言，令愛面子的爸爸屢動肝火。「每次有街坊問他，花舍是否捱不往之後，他都會回來破口大罵：『你睇，花店沒有花，似咩樣？』」兩代交烽火花四濺，但遺傳了爸爸固執性格的Betty堅持己見，終成功節流。

即使爸爸相對保守，心底還是很支持年輕人作不同嘗試。「他覺得，既然能騰出空間，也不妨借出來給年輕人推廣他們的產品。」Betty把花舍逾半面積變作寄賣區，擅長櫥窗佈置的丈夫阿康更一顯身手，引入多個本地手作品牌，兼賣文創精品。

Betty本來對花藝一竅不通，便報名上堂，閒時請教同行，慢慢愛上了插花。「我是個很大情大性的人，而插花總能令我心平氣和下來。」她也鍾情於花店所帶來的鄰里關係，以及對未來的想像。「花舍不賺錢，但將來孩子來了，便有空間供他們跑來跑去，我還可以親手帶大他們呢。」Betty抱著貓店長，眉開眼笑地說。

福

長洲花舍

A FLOWER SHOP WITH NO FLOWERS:
Cheung Chau Garden

Papa Siu takes pride in being a jack-of-all-trades businessman. He has got his hands on eight different industries: "I have sold pork, beef, Cantonese barbecue, electronics, fruits, and tried fish-farming. Now I run the restaurant and this flower shop." After his daughter Betty was born, Papa Siu felt the need to find an alternative source of income, hence launching Cheung Chau Garden the next year.

"Do you know why I switched from being a butcher to a florist?" Papa Siu asks. "That's because nobody sold flowers here at that time." Merely a matter of opportunity, there was no romantic reason behind the first flower shop on the island.

The flower shop has a history of 30 years, while the meat stall and the restaurant have been on track for decades. But the seasoned businessman had also ridden through storms over the years.

"The electronic store on Mui Wo had to shut within two months of its opening, and I lost HK$270,000," he recalls. "It was coincidental with the opening of the new wet market. With the costs required for the meat stall's set-up and bidding fees, we ran into a cash flow problem. I didn't want to borrow money from others, so I just filled my stomach with two bowls of plain noodles every day."

Papa Siu has subsequently become more cautious in his investments. "This pandemic has proven me right. Even though the catering industry has been the first to bear the brunt, the restaurant remains quite stable to date."

Cheung Chau Garden had only one staff member who did not know much about floristry when it first opened. An affiliated florist would travel to the island with fresh flowers by appointment, complete the orders at the shop and catch the ferry back to the city right after. Having observed the florist's work, that staffer and Papa Siu gradually learned the basic techniques, and it was only then that the shop began to have flower bouquets for retail.

On the day when the shop reopened after the Lunar New Year break in 2015, the only staff member suddenly quit because she had to take care of her grandchild. Papa Siu couldn't find a replacement and was prepared to shut the shop. But Betty did not want her father's years of efforts to go in vain, so she took over.

Betty, who went to Britain for studies at 13 years old, confesses that the decision was not easy. "I initially planned to pursue a master's degree, but my mom fell sick, so I returned as soon as I finished my undergraduate." Two years later, her mother passed away, and Betty, who had a full-time marketing job for a year, decided to return to school for a food science programme. So she pursued her master's while taking care of the flower shop at the same time.

After she took over, Betty was surprised to discover that the shop had been operating at a loss over the years. "Flowers wither after two to three days. More flowers were thrown out than sold." Seeing that 80-90% of the business came from pre-orders, she decisively resumed the earlier model of not having flowers in stock, but only placed orders for flowers after receiving customers' purchases. "The shop couldn't keep losing money just for maintaining a fanciful window display."

However, this radical change stirred rumours of closure and angered Papa Siu, who is sensitive about reputation. "Every time someone asked him whether the flower shop was about to close, he would come back and yell at me: 'You see, a flower shop without flowers. How bad it looks!'" The two had heated debates, but Betty, who is just as stubborn as her father, insisted on her decision and finally managed to cut costs.

Though Papa Siu is relatively conservative, he is very supportive of young people trying new things. "He thought that since we could make room anyway, we might as well lend it to young people to promote their products." Betty thus turned half of the shop's space into a consignment area for local handmade brands.

Betty originally knew nothing about floristry, so she took classes and learned from other florists during her free time, and slowly developed a love for floral arrangement. "I tend to get emotional easily, and floral arrangement always calms me down." She also adores the sense of community brought by the shop and cannot picture a future without it. "Perhaps the flower shop is not profitable, but it would be the space for children to run around when they come." Betty holds one of the store cats in her arms and says with a smile: "I will then devote all my time to bringing them up."

又合號 Yau Hap Ho

又合號
莫道桑榆晚 為霞尚滿天

又合號的蕭先生是上文長洲花舍蕭爸爸的哥哥；兩兄弟都曾在店工作，弟弟後來轉行開花店，哥哥繼續開肉檔；兩兄弟，兩種不同的生活態度。

蕭先生生於1945年2月，半年後的8月15日，日軍無條件投降，結束了香港「三年零八個月」的淪陷時期。他笑言：「街坊都叫我做『光仔』，因為我生下來沒多久後香港就重光了。」

戰後百廢待興，地主有見居民生活艱難，便捐出東灣路廣場的一大塊空地作公眾街市。現已拆卸的長安街市分四段，一共六十四檔，鮮肉、海鮮、蔬菜、雜貨各十六檔，只象徵性收費十元月租。不少街坊也想經營小生意，故反應踴躍，最後以抽籤方式決定，而蕭生的爸爸因有屠宰經驗而順利投得其中一檔。

在糧食短缺的情況下，蕭生回憶起一家人胼手胝足的日子。「小時沒有自來水，我六七歲便開始幫忙擔水洗豬，大一點便開始負責送貨。」當時有不少孩子因營養不良而早逝，蕭生一家全賴肉枱賣剩的頭頭尾尾，才得溫飽。「那時沒有雪櫃，豬肉在室溫放上一整天後不免會發臭，媽媽便下大量蒜蓉豆豉辟味，加上隔離檔的菜頭菜尾，養活了我們十兄弟姊妹。」

長洲居民多利用門前的空地飼養牲口，蕭家會四出找合適的豬隻入購。「每家人多數也有兩三隻豬，而我們專找的中型豬，四五個月便達一百至百二斤。」蕭生爸爸每晚會把豬隻帶到後院宰豬，由蕭生媽媽按着豬隻，「因六點左右開檔，所以會待凌晨三四時才宰豬。臨終前的動物會掙扎、會嚎叫。每晚也吵着鄰居，回想起來真的好抱歉。」

十六歲時，蕭生決定離島闖闖，到紗廠打工。紗廠除了包食宿，下午六時下班後更可上夜校進修，對於一直渴望讀書上學的他，無疑理想不過。「有天吃過午飯後，陽光斜下，微塵飄飄浮浮。我才驚覺空氣中有好多幼細的粒子，不知對健康有什麼影響。」離開工廠後，他又到麵包店當學徒，直至二十三歲時，爸爸積勞成疾，他才回歸重執起刀來，三十歲才正式接手。

隨着經濟騰飛，街坊消費時漸漸闊綽，令鮮肉需求大增，蕭生的肉枱擴充至三個檔口，但他拒絕當守財奴。「我這一生，只愛兩個女人，我的母親和我的妻子。」蕭生是不折不扣的愛妻號，不諱言善於長線計劃的妻子對他影響深遠。有一天，太太和蕭生坐下來，好好談談他們的將來。她說，既然各有穩定收入，育兒供樓綽綽有餘，就不用一年到晚都營營役役。「就這樣，我便在長洲開了先河，成為首家只經營半天的豬肉檔。」Work-life balance 要到四五十年後的今天才漸受關注，足見太太的高瞻遠矚。

蕭生和太太年少相識時已喜歡結伴露營旅行，而縮短營業時間後，每年至少會有一個十至二十天的悠長假期，以及三數次短途旅行。而除了踏遍萬里路，蕭生又嚮往讀萬卷書，彌補兒時教育匱乏的遺憾。

剛屆耄耋之年的他說：「我這生人，真的沒什麼大志。」退休後，除了卷不離手，最喜歡與朋友把酒言歡。「每一個人都獨一無二，每一個人都有自己的故事。每一次交談，都是彼此學習。」蕭生的電話總是響過不停，全是飲茶喝酒的邀約。他打趣自己是「先施」的代言人：「先付出、先施予，才有回應。縱使未必即時察覺，但總有得著。」

99.0元
68.0元
牛坑腩 100元

Yau Hap Ho: **A POST-WAR BUTCHER'S STALL**

Mr. Siu is the elder brother of Papa Siu of Cheung Chau Garden. While Papa Siu went on to explore different trades, Mr. Siu stayed at the meat stall of their parents.

Mr. Siu was born in February 1945. Half a year later, Japan announced its unconditional surrender, thus ending its three years and eight months of occupation of Hong Kong. He jokes: "My neighbours all called me Gwong Zai, as Hong Kong was liberated soon after I was born."

Seeing how difficult people's lives were after the Second World War, a landlord donated a large piece of land at the Tung Wan Road Plaza to build a wet market for the public. The now demolished Cheung On Wet Market was divided into four sections—fresh meat, seafood, vegetables and dry goods, each with 16 stalls. Tenants would only be charged a monthly fee of HK$10. Many locals were eager to start their businesses and successful applications were decided by drawing lots in the end. With previous experience in butchering, Mr. Siu's father was allotted one without much trouble.

Facing a shortage in food supply, Mr. Siu remembers how his family was burning the candle at both ends during that time. "As there was no tap water, I helped carry buckets of water to rinse the pigs when I was six or seven years old. I started helping with deliveries once I was older."

Many children died of malnutrition in those days, but the Siu family was able to feed themselves with scraps of leftovers from their stalls. "There was no refrigerator back then. Cuts of pork would start to stink after being kept at room temperature for the entire day," he recalls. "My mom would use a lot of garlic and douchi in her cooking to hide the smell. Along with the scraps from other stalls, she was able to feed all ten kids in our family."

Cheung Chau locals usually raised livestock in the empty space in front of their homes, so the Siu family often ventured out to seek suitable pigs for buying. "Each family owned two to three pigs, but we were looking for medium-sized pigs only. After four to five months, they could weigh up to 100 to 120 kg." Every night, Mr. Siu's father would bring the pigs to the backyard and his mom would hold them down. "We opened our store at around 6 a.m., so we would wait till 3 or 4 a.m. to butcher the pigs. They struggled and screeched before they took their last breath," he says. "Now that I think about it, I feel sorry for my neighbours, we really were disturbing them every night."

When he was 16, Mr. Siu decided to leave for the city and worked at a mill. Apart from covering their meals and accommodation, it also subsidised staff to study at night school. It was the ideal job for Mr. Siu, who had always wanted to go to school. Until one day after lunch, he saw many dust particles floating in the air under the sun.

"At that moment, I suddenly realised that the air was full of many tiny molecules, and I didn't even know how they would affect my health." After leaving the mill, he worked as an apprentice at a bakery. His father fell ill because of constant overwork when Mr. Siu was 23. It was only by then that he returned to Cheung Chau to pick up the butcher's knife. By the age of 30, Mr. Siu officially took over the business.

As the economy took off, more and more locals could afford fresh meat. Mr. Siu's butcher business expanded to three storefronts, but he refused to be a money-grubber. "In my whole life, I have only loved two women. One is my mother, and the other is my wife." Mr. Siu truly adores his wife, who is good at long-term planning. One day, his wife sat down with him and started talking about their future.

Now that they had stable incomes, she said, they could afford to support their mortgage and raise their children. Hence, they no longer needed to overwork themselves on a daily basis. "And just like that, I became the first butcher to adopt half-day working on Cheung Chau." The emphasis on work-life balance—something that is only widely valued nowadays—proves his wife's foresight a good half-century ago.

When they were young, Mr. Siu and his wife loved to go camping together. The shortening of business hours allowed them to enjoy at least 10 to 12 days of holiday and three short trips every year. Besides travelling, Mr. Siu is an avid reader. It is his own way of making up for the limited access to education when he was a child.

Now in his 80s, Mr. Siu says he doesn't have much ambition in life. Upon retirement, he splits his time between reading and hanging out with his friends over a couple of beers. "Every person is unique, every person has their own stories. Every time we talk, we learn from each other." Mr. Siu's phone is always ringing, inviting him to yum chai or get a drink.

He shares his wisdom of giving: "Only by being the first to give, that people will respond to you. Even though you may not notice, you will always get something in return."

by Samson Cheung

長洲長櫈

Benches and Branches

長洲本來就是綠色社區的典範。街上沒有汽車，來往各處就只靠單車和雙腳。山丘佔這座小島很大面積，所以大部份住屋依山而建，居民每日來來回回，上山落山。

作為遊客，每條上山的路上每隔一小段總會有長櫈讓我停下來享受寧靜，欣賞美景；作為居民，特別是公公婆婆，拖著沉重的購物車，長櫈是重要的中途站讓他們可以小休一會，然後繼續上路。

一個可以讓人放慢、停靠的空間，哪怕微小如一張路邊椅子，卻蘊藏生活的本質。

Cheung Chau has always been the model of a green community—there are no cars on the streets, people travel to places by bike or on foot. A large portion of the island is made up of hills, so most housing is built along the hillsides and people need to traverse up and downhill every day.

For visiting tourists, there are benches on each uphill path for taking breaks and enjoying the serene, scenic views. For the islanders, especially the seniors lugging along heavy shopping carts, these benches are essential pit stops before continuing on to their next destination.

A roadside bench may seem insignificant, but as a space that allows for slowing down and resting, it is part of our lives.

Chapter 04

第四章

Crafts

藝

長洲是傳統的，也是年輕的，而難得地，兩者並不互相排斥，而是平等共存。在長洲，總能輕易見到島上的新舊共融。打醮時有手紮麒麟頭帶隊巡遊；平日走在街上可見到螢光手寫花牌；逛不同小店，又見到別出心裁的創意設計。除了普遍較市區低廉的租金降低小店創業門檻外，長洲獨有的自然光風、歷史文化、社群氛圍、生活方式等，孕育出島民的創意和手藝。最後一章，我們訪問長洲不同年紀的創作人，細看長洲的文化底蘊。

Cheung Chau is home to both the old and the young, the traditional and the contemporary. Besides traditional paper-crafted qilin heads that lead the procession at every Da Jiu Festival, the streets are often lined with handmade neon signages and different small shops that feature their quaint designs. Thanks to its relatively affordable rent, Cheung Chau has facilitated and inspired the creativity and crafts of many. In the final chapter, Cheung Chau creatives of different ages give us a closer look at the cultural heritage of the island.

11
NOVEMBER

友聯廣告

Yau Luen Advertising

友聯廣告
街頭螢光花牌學

今時今日，大家心裡有什麼說話都寫上社交媒體，但在長洲，事無大小，由太平清醮和誕期，到某某聯婚、社團通告、新店開張，以至隔壁黃太生日，都會以花牌祝賀，尤其是有新店開張時，店外整條街都是螢光色的花牌，有如街頭版的Facebook feed。

陳愛民師傅是島上首家製作螢光花牌的「友聯廣告」的第二代接班人。友聯由陳師傅的父親陳松友於1967年創立，當時島上只有大型活動才會製作紙紮花牌，由一間名為福興隆的紙紮舖包辦，但舊式花牌製作需時，於是原本任校工並寫得一手好字的陳父，便膽粗粗開始花牌生意，首創直立式花牌，手寫靚字配鮮艷顏色，「他做廣告這一行，一定要搶眼。」起初老一輩對陳父的新式花牌並不受落，經過一年多才接受，「要慢慢滲入去（長洲），用平價打入市場……加上爸爸在長洲出世，跟社團熟絡，便嘗試找他做花牌。」

久而久之，花牌成為長洲特色，現時島上有兩間製作花牌的公司，天保主白事，友聯主紅事。友聯的舖位隱身於民居中，店內層架放滿了寫上不同字句的紙條，紙條用螢光筆塗滿底色，配以粗黑雙頭筆的手寫大字，原來這些是多年來儲下來的「預製組件」，譬如有新店開張，「開張大吉」、「生意興隆」等賀詞都已有齊，他只需補上款和下款便可。製成後陳師傅和伙記會把花牌送到店舖，一般四、五日後收回，把樣板放回原位，下次再用，他笑言：「好聽是環保，唔好聽是做得快。」

一塊開張的花牌八十蚊，多字一點的通告也只需二、三百，幾個鐘便能起貨。陳師傅說，在長洲做花牌，最緊要平、靚、正，密密做才有錢賺。雖不是什麼精雕細琢的工藝，卻以效率取勝，迎合長洲人的需要，「長洲很多社團，他們每年幾個活動，收得貴的話人們負擔不起。」除了社團，近年也多了人以大型棚架花牌宣布婚訊。

話說回頭，陳師傅十幾歲就在舖頭幫手，但中學後便到香港工作，沒想過以花牌為志業。直到十幾年前，父親過世，決定接手生意，他說得輕淡：「其實都幾大轉變，但見有檔生意，爸爸剩下來的，便試吓接手。」但他無意傳給下一代：「又辛苦，又賺唔到錢，為什麼要傳下去？」製作花牌看似手板眼見工夫，但也睇天做人。有些大花牌需要搭棚，也是由友聯包辦，「試過兩天後便是活動開幕，但開幕前總是落雨，也要『焗住』去做。」遇着打風前夕也是兩難，貿然拆棚會被客人罵，如果不拆又怕有危險。但安全起見，一般都會拆掉。

多年來，陳師傅製作的花牌多不勝數，最滿意的莫過於早幾年為太平清醮重新設計的巨型花牌。每年打醮，現場都會搭起棚架，架上宏偉複雜的花牌，幾年前，主辦單位希望換掉沿用了二、三十年的花牌，於是陳師傅花幾個月時間設計和製作，「新的清醮花牌形態像一間廟。」雖辛苦，但聽得出師傅的自豪。

動筆之際，長洲興隆正街有新食店開張，附近的巷子豎了好幾十個花牌，好不張揚，假如在市區，這些花牌想必被指阻街，但在長洲，只要不阻礙別人出入就不成問題，「所謂家家有求，他日你開張，也想有人送花牌祝賀吧！」陳師傅說。這就是長洲人的默契。

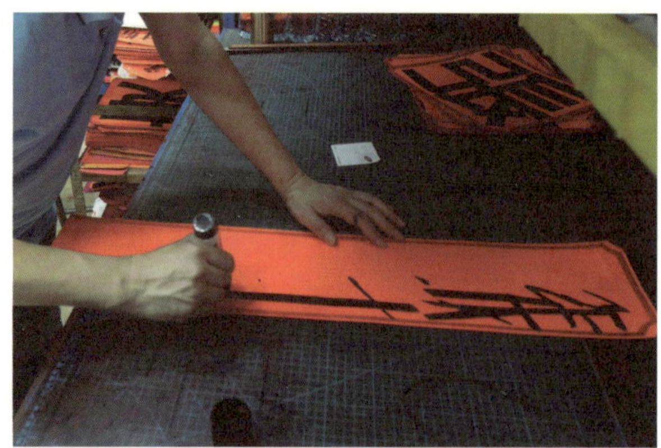

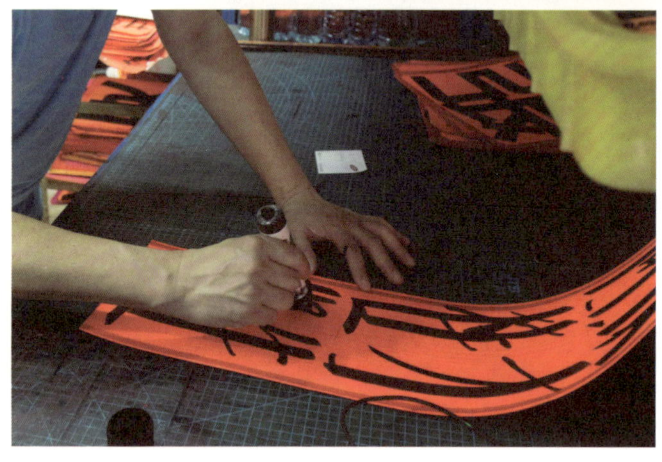

prohibited
t handcarts
midnight
holiday
夜十二時
全日
進入
身體.心靈.平靜
生活.輕鬆.自在
Simplyog
Cheung Chau Island
6253 2253
9330 8057
新興街97號2樓
2/f 97, San Hing Street
Simplyog
Simplyogcc
東莞會所
頒發獎助學金
電話: 2981 3225
(歡迎外賣或訂座)
長洲新興後街185號地下
弘廚
西式餐廳
Wang Kitchen
營業時間:
早上7:30-下午3:00
晚上6:00-晚上9:30
逢星期四休息
醒神早餐
悠閒午餐

wonderful maestros
history and everything
we are waiting
博愛
Pok Oi Hospit
博愛醫院
長洲中醫服務
地址
長洲教堂路2號
長洲鄉事委員會2樓
預約
通知會員友好
經本會商議後決定
取消本年度會員大會
東煌麵館
地道車仔麵
鎮店三寶
地址：長洲大新後
電話查
(852) 2889 6513

Yau Luen Advertising: **NEON FLOWER BOARDS ACROSS STREETS AND ALLEYS**

Nowadays we often take our views to social media, but on Cheung Chau, all things big and small—from the Bun Festival to weddings, community notices, shop openings, and even birthdays—are announced on flower boards. This is especially the case whenever a new store launches, the entire street of its location would be lined with neon flower boards, just like a Facebook feed materialised on the streets.

Chan Oi Man is the second-generation owner of Yau Luen Advertising — the island's first neon flower board production company. Yau Luen was established by his father Chan Chung Yau in 1967. Traditional paper flower boards, primarily for large-scale events at that time, were made by a paper offering shop called Fook Hing Lung and the production was time-consuming. So Chan's father, who was originally a school janitor with superb handwriting, boldly launched his own flower board business. He pioneered the vertical flower board design by pairing beautifully handwritten calligraphy with vibrant colours. "It is important to be eye-catching in advertising," he notes.

The older generations were initially not a fan of his father's flower boards, and it took over a year for them to accept the new style. "It took time to break into the Cheung Chau market with a cheap price... Also my father was born on Cheung Chau, so he was close to some of the local associations who gave his flower boards a try."

Over time, the flower board has become a unique feature of Cheung Chau. Currently, there are two flower board production companies: Tin Bo focuses on funeral events, and Yau Luen specialises in celebratory occasions.

Yau Luen's store is tucked in the residential area. The shelves inside are stacked with paper slips written with various kinds of phrases. The banners are painted over with highlighters, on which big words are written with dual-tip black markers. These are the "pre-prepared parts" that have been reused over the years. For example, for the occasion of a new store opening, phrases like "Grand Opening" and "Brisk Business" come in handy, and the only words that need to be added are the names of the recipient and the sender. Once the board is done, Mr. Chan and his staff would deliver the board to the store, and collect it after four or five days. The template would be saved for the next order. He jokes, "You can say that it's environmentally friendly, or it's simply efficient."

A flower board for a store opening costs about HK$80, and a notice with more customised words only charges HK$200-300, and all can be produced within several hours. As Mr. Chan explains, if one wants to make a profit from flower board production on Cheung Chau, one has to produce cheap but beautiful boards, and make a lot of them. It is not a craft that requires delicate precision, but something that can be made efficiently to fulfill customers' needs. "There are many associations on Cheung Chau and each has several events every year, they cannot afford it if it's too expensive." Besides associations, more and more people have used large-scale scaffolding flower boards for wedding announcements in recent years.

Looking back, Mr. Chan began to work at the store when he was just a teenager. He left the island to work in the city after finishing secondary school, and never thought of pursuing a career in the flower board business. It was not until about ten years ago when his father had passed away that he decided to take over. He says: "Actually it was quite a big change. But looking at this business that my father had left behind, I thought I'd give it a try."

However, he has no intention to pass it on to the next generation. "It's a tough job and it does not make much money. Why pass it down?" Making flower boards might seem to be a simple hands-on task, but it also depends a lot on the weather. Some giant flower boards require scaffolding, which is also taken care of by Yau Luen. "One time it kept raining just two days before an event opening and we had no choice but to keep going." A dilemma also arises usually on the night before a typhoon hits: either Mr. Chan risks angering the client if they remove the scaffolding altogether, or they risk the danger of collapse by keeping it on. Usually, the scaffolding would be removed for safety's sake.

Mr. Chan has produced countless flower boards over the years, but the one that he is most satisfied with is the enormous flower board that he redesigned for the Bun Festival a couple of years ago. Every year during the Bun Festival, scaffoldings are built on site with a grand and complex flower board hung over top. The organisers wanted to replace the 20- to 30-year-old flower boards, so Mr. Chan spent a few months designing and producing them. "The new Bun Festival flower board is the shape of a temple." It was a tough job, and one can hear the craftsman's pride in his voice.

At the time of penning this article, a new restaurant opened on Hing Lung Main Street, and more than 30 flower boards stood on the alley next to it, creating a spectacle. If this scenery takes place in the city, the flower boards will be regarded as street obstruction. On Cheung Chau however, it is never a problem as long as the boards do not block others' way. "Everybody has a need someday. One day when you open your store, you'd probably also want others to send you celebratory flower boards!" And this speaks to the mutual understanding shared by the people of Cheung Chau.

藝術家杜煥

Sugarman

藝術家杜煥
承繼傳統工藝

面前是一兜溶掉的糖漿，藝術家用竹簽挑起一團，像挑麥芽糖一樣，再將之拉長，足足有一米多，拉出一條幼管，他的女兒用口向細管的末端緩緩吹氣，糖球愈吹愈大，之後他用剪刀在半硬的糖球表面又剪又拉，不出幾分鐘便成了一條生猛的糖龍。他叫杜煥，人稱 Sugarman，糖人。

杜煥的小店開在碼頭附近大廣場的一角，該處人流暢旺，但近年很少見他的店開門做生意，長期只見一道畫滿畫的鐵閘，神神秘秘，「唔憂做」似的，他經常強調：「我只志在喺長洲有啲嘢玩吓。」話雖如此，他對待自己的手藝卻絕不「玩玩吓」。原本專注繪畫和雕塑的他，2000 年搬到長洲，他笑言當時自己留了一把長及臀部的頭髮，像個「死臭飛」，想不到業主也願意租給他，一住便二十年。一搬到島，他便發覺長洲有不少他的潮洲同鄉，令他分外有親切感，他亦到處探索長洲，包括島上的傳統文化，「這裡的傳統文化跟我故鄉的很接近，可惜鄉下很多東西在文化大革命時被破壞，但在長洲仍保留到。」

直到 2005 年長洲復辦搶包山，長洲遊客大增，啓發他以傳統元素進行創作，並於 2009 年開店，售賣自家設計的產品，把包山、神像等圖像印在布袋、T-shirt 等產品上，「當時沒有本地人敢購買，他們覺得太詭異，但外國人卻很喜歡。」

之後，他再踩深一腳，不只是用傳統元素創作，而是縱身鑽研傳統糖塑，「我自小已經很喜歡糖公仔，五、六歲時在故鄉，躲在師傅身後偷看他們怎樣製作，用對眼偷師。」後來因股災，加上妻子懷孕，糖人生活較清閒，便着手研究他一直很懷念的糖塑，摸索配方。糖塑的原料是米芽糖，成分跟麥芽糖差無幾，但前者顏色通透。糖人一邊製作一邊解釋：「氣溫會影響糖的軟硬度，冬天的時候要半分鐘內做起一隻公仔，否則糖就會變硬。」

一開頭他自問功夫未到家，不敢大肆宣揚，只在小店中五蚊一隻出售，後來妻子拿出街上賣，轉個頭便賣清。於是糖人加緊操練，客人想要什麼公仔──龍、鳳、猴、蛇、鳥，都要做到。他的糖塑技藝更揚威海外，在歐洲獲當地電視台訪問。但他絕不是有求必應，「有人要我做比卡超，我不會做，我不是要做整糖機械人，也不想做別人的東西。」

訪問期間，有幾個路過的小學生說：「這糖公仔我食過啊！好玩啊！」也有上了年紀的叔叔讚賞：「很難得仲有人做。」糖人指早年開檔，一日可賺幾萬蚊，但近年，一日都賣不到十蚊，他現時主要是大時大節才開店，「想為長洲增加多一個元素。」除了拉糖公仔外，他也會做傳統紮作，早兩年太平清醮的麒麟頭便是他的傑作，他更首次加入防水物料，改良傳統做法，「潛水都得！」

在長洲住了二十年，他跟很多老街坊一樣，感慨長洲的租金隨住人流增加而上升，人與人的關係也隨生活忙碌而變疏，「以前這廣場總是坐着一班阿婆在搣咸魚。」但他仍然覺得長洲，這個他一世人住得最久的小島，是個好地方：「長洲人好多事都有得傾，不會一下要置你於死地，人無咁壞。」

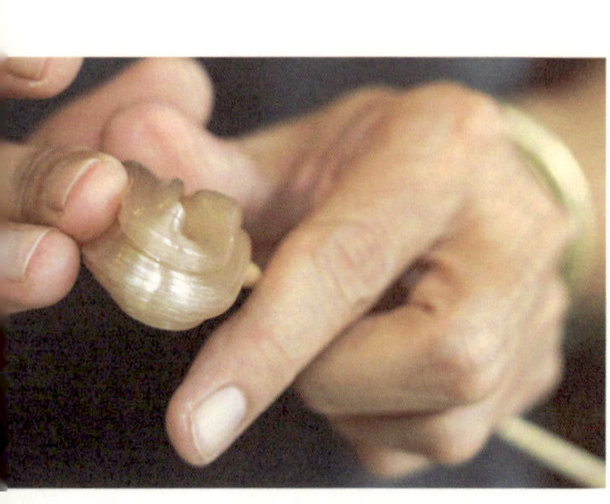

STICK IT ON!
Defend Our City

糖
7up
Fresh Up with 7up
7up
Fragrant

Sugarman: **MODERNISING A TRADITIONAL CRAFT**

Set in front of the artist is a bowl of melted sugar, To Wun uses a bamboo cane to lift a pool of maltose syrup, pulling and stretching until it is almost one-metre long. He then pulls out a thin hollow tube and his daughter slowly blows through it to create a ball of sugar that grows bigger and bigger. With a pair of scissors, he cuts and pulls the half-hard ball, forming a ferocious sugar dragon in no time. The artist To Wun is also as known as *tong yan*, the Sugarman.

To Wun's shop nestles at the corner of the plaza near the pier, where it is almost always bustling with activities. But his shop is rarely open for business in recent years. For a long while, all we can see are the many paintings on their metal gates, as if making a profit is not his concern.

As the artist often says, he "only wants to have something to play with on Cheung Chau." That said, he definitely is not playing around with his crafts. To Wun initially placed his creative focus on drawing and sculpture. When he moved to Cheung Chau in 2000, he had hair long enough to reach his butt. "It probably gave me the look of a delinquent", he pokes fun at himself looking back. But lucky enough, he still managed to find a flat and has since been living on Cheung Chau for 20 years.

His bond with the island grew deeper especially after he discovered that many locals were too from his original hometown, Chiuchow. He also went around to explore Cheung Chau. "The traditions here are highly similar to that of my hometown, most of which were destroyed during the Cultural Revolution unfortunately. But, Cheung Chau was able to preserve them."

The reintroduction of the bun towers and the bun-snatching ritual in 2005 prompted a surge in tourists. This inspired To Wun to use traditional elements in his creative practice. In 2009, he started selling his own designs, incorporating the motifs of bun towers and deities in souvenirs such as tote bags and t-shirts. "At that time no locals would think of buying them, they found them too freakish, but foreigners loved them."

He then went the extra mile in exploring traditional motifs. Not only did he include them in his works, he also immersed himself in the study and making of sugar figurines. "I developed a liking for sugar sculpture from a young age," he says. "Back in my hometown, when I was still five or six years old, I would observe behind the back of the craftsmen when they made sugar figurines. I tried to learn the techniques with my eyes."

After the stock markets crashed and his wife got pregnant, the artist had more spare time and started researching the making of sugar figurines that he had sorely missed. The primary material of his recipe is rice syrup, which is very similar to maltose but transparent in colour. He explains as he keeps on working, "The temperature affects how hard or soft the sugar is. During winter, you sometimes need to finish a figurine within half a minute, or else the sugar would already harden."

At first, To Wun felt that he had yet to excel in the sugar-pulling techniques and did not want to publicise his business. His figurines were only priced at HK$5 each at the shop. However, they were gone within seconds once his wife started selling them on the streets. He thus worked even harder to perfect his craft, so that he could create whatever figurines his customers wanted—dragons, phoenixes, monkeys, snakes, or birds. His craftsmanship soon won him the name "Sugarman" and he was even interviewed by a European television channel after gaining fame overseas.

However, he does not make everything his customers request. "Someone asked me to create a Pikachu figurine but I refused. I am not a sugar sculpture-making machine, and I don't want to replicate characters created by others either."

During our interview, several primary students passing by say: "I have eaten this sugar figurine before! It's really fun!" An elderly man also expresses his appreciation, "It is really hard to find someone still doing this now." Sugarman says he could make thousands of dollars in one day by selling sugar figurines a few years ago, but now he cannot even make HK$10 a day.

Now his shop is only open during public holidays or festivals. "I want to add another element to Cheung Chau." Apart from making sugar figurines, he also works on paper crafting. The qilin head of the ritual dance for the Bun Festival several years ago was his proud creation. It was his first time experimenting with waterproof materials, thereby refining the traditional craft. "You can even scuba dive with it!"

Like many of his old neighbours, To Wun too feels that the rent has gone up and residents have grown estranged from each other as life gets busier over the past two decades. "Back then, there was always a group of grannies sitting in the plaza shredding salted fish." Despite all the changes, he still finds Cheung Chau, where he has lived for the longest period, a great place. "You can always talk and figure things out with the people here. They will never push you into a corner. People on Cheung Chau are not bad."

畫家楊長明

Yeung Cheung Ming

畫家楊長明
廁紙上的工筆畫

新興街[1]曾經有一間雜貨店，店前陳列出主要是毛巾和廁紙的商品，店長楊長明架着眼鏡坐在店前，他的身後則是大批大批的貨物，堆積如山。這間店看似不修邊幅，店主楊生卻是中國畫高手，有時見他總是低頭苦幹，並不是他故意冷漠，而可能是他正在專心地抄一行如米粒般大的詩句，或者畫一隻肉眼難辨的小螞蟻。

楊生自小從香港搬到長洲，在長洲成長，對畫畫有強烈興趣，早年以畫瓷器維生，後來轉為紙上繪畫，精通多種技法。訪問當日，他帶來多幅作品，並逐一介紹：只有黑白線條，繪畫佛教人物維摩向眾人講義的《維摩演教圖》，畫法是白描；畫上青綠山巒的是「青綠山水」技法，以石青、石綠的礦物提取出青綠色，一座山塗了八層顏色；還有一幅是幾個孩童在放紙鳶，而細看繫着紙鳶的線，原來是一行微型字！幅幅作品都維肖維妙，他滿意地指：「無畫家有我畫種咁闊。」

他又用手機向我展示一幅即將在大會堂展出的界畫作品《梁園飛雪》，界畫是中國畫的一種，繪畫時用界尺引線，多用於精密複雜的建築物，最著名的界畫為《清明上河圖》。楊生指，這類畫很考耐性，現在很少人識畫，而這樣一幅畫，他就要畫幾個月。

除了巨幅畫作，他也總是隨身帶着碎紙、報紙、紙巾、廁紙，隨時隨地即席揮毫，而且無論紙張有多細小，都難不到他的妙筆。他指：「宣紙、玉扣紙、絹紙，咩紙我都可以畫，甚至廁紙都可以。」在廁紙上作畫不是貪過癮，而是有實際功用，尤其是用毛筆，他解釋：「用廁紙畫畫可以練習速度，假如畫得慢，紙就會被墨穿透，變濕及穿窿，所以要同張紙鬥快！當試過很多不同厚薄度的紙之後，支筆就可以做到好輕、好飄，日後可以畫到好幼細的畫。別人追求『力透紙背』，我就相反，講求點到即止。」作畫如做人，但求做到輕重收放自如。

自學成材的他，為了精進畫藝，不時到古董店和拍賣行參考他人的作品，又會看書研究畫的源流，哪個時期哪個畫家最出色，譬如他指宋朝宋徽宗時期設立畫院，因而培訓了不少出色畫師。直至現在，他仍會每晚畫一至兩小時畫，他慨嘆道：「反觀現在，世界以經濟先行，畫畫只是殺時間，不會有太多人有錢去支持畫家。」他亦曾經在長洲教畫，在店內開張檯，邊做生意邊教畫，他自言是個嚴師，從不會幫學生改畫，要他們自己學習。對於畫，他有自己的堅持：「我畫畫不是為求名利，如果跟我有緣的，我可以不收分毫送畫，無緣的話，多多錢都不賣。」即使有人向他訂畫，也要給他十足自由度，除了尺吋之外，其他都由畫家發揮，「我就係我，唔洗理人，像趙少昂的鈐印『我之為我，自有我在』[2]。」

1 店舖其後搬到新興後街
2 「我之為我 自有我在」原句出自清初畫家石濤，趙少昂借用刻成刻章印在其畫上。

Yeung Cheung Ming: **GONGBI PAINTING ON TOILET PAPER**

There was once a grocery shop on Sun Hing Street[1] that mainly displayed products like towels and toilet rolls. Its bespectacled shop owner Yeung Cheung Ming usually sits at the shopfront, with piles and piles of goods stacked up like a hill behind him. The owner of this seemingly messy shop is also a Chinese painting master. He is often seen working hard with his head kept down, which must not be mistaken as a sign of neglect—perhaps he is just concentrating on copying a line of poetry with characters as small as rice grains or painting an ant that could hardly be identified with the naked eye.

Mr. Yeung moved to Cheung Chau from Hong Kong when he was a child. Growing up on the island, he has had a strong passion for painting since a young age. In the early years, he would make a living by painting porcelain wares, only switching to painting on paper later. He is adept in multiple painting techniques.

On the day of the interview, he brings along a pile of his works and introduces them one by one. For works painted in only black strokes of ink and resembling figure paintings like *Vimalakīrti Preaching Buddhist Doctrine*, they are done in the baimiao ("plain drawing") technique. Landscape paintings in blue and green contain colours extracted from azurite blue and malachite green, and a mountain is composed of eight layers of colours. Another work depicts several children flying their kites, but if you inspect the strings of the kites closely, you will spot miniature lines of Chinese characters. Each work is a piece of marvel. Mr. Yeung says: "No other painter can paint in as many genres as I do."

One of his works to be exhibited at the Hong Kong City Hall is a *Jiehua* ("ruled line") painting named *Flying Snow at Liang's Garden*. *Jiehua* is a genre of traditional Chinese painting, in which the painter would meticulously depict architecture and sceneries with the aid of a ruler. The most famous work of this genre is *Along the River During the Qingming Festival*. According to Mr. Yeung, this genre requires much patience, and each painting can take several months to complete.

Apart from creating large pieces of work, Mr. Yeung always carries around some scrap paper like newspaper and tissue paper for him to paint on at anytime and anywhere. "Be it Xuan paper, Yukou paper or silk paper...I can paint on any kind of paper, even on toilet paper."

Painting on toilet paper is not something he does on a whim. In fact, it has a practical purpose, especially when he paints with an ink brush. "You can train your painting speed when working on toilet paper," he explains. "If you paint too slowly, the ink will fully soak through the paper, leaving it too wet and torn with holes. That's why you need to race against the paper! Once you've tried paper with different thicknesses, you can achieve a lightness with your pen and excel in drawing extremely fine lines."

"Others strive for having enough 'calligraphic force to penetrate the paper,' I am the opposite, looking to stop at the right level." He paints with the same attitude as he leads his life, hoping to exert and absorb all matters in life with flexibility.

As a self-taught artist, he frequents antique shops and preview exhibitions of auction houses to study other artworks and reads up on the historical development of every genre. Until today, Mr. Yeung still spends one to two hours every evening on painting.

"The world today is driven by economic factors. Painting is only a way to kill time; not too many people are willing to support painters financially." He once taught painting on Cheung Chau, setting aside a table in his shop to teach while doing business. He claims to be a strict teacher who never corrects his students' works directly, as he wants them to learn on their own.

When it comes to painting, he adheres to his principles.

"I paint neither for fame nor wealth. I could give a work away without taking a single penny if I feel like it. If not, I wouldn't sell a work no matter how much I'm being offered."

He insists on having absolute freedom even for commissioned works, so that he can experiment with all aspects of the work besides its dimensions. "I am me after all. I pay no heed to others' expectations, just like the seal of Shao'ang says: 'I am as I am; I exist.'[2]"

1 Yeung's shop was later moved to Sun Hing Back Street.

2 "I am as I am; I exist" was originally written by early Qing dynasty painter Shitao. Zhao Shao'ang borrowed this phrase and had it carved as an artist's seal for his painting

DAY FERRY
NICK FLO

唱作人 Nick Florent

Another Day On The Ferry

唱作人 Nick Florent
一隻給長洲的唱片

第一次見到 Nick 的唱片，是在西灣的酒吧餐廳海盜灣。那張唱片封套畫上熟悉的長洲風景——一艘正在埋岸的新渡輪，碟名為 Another Day on the Ferry，一看便知是長洲出品。回家找歌來聽，有力的藍調結他，伴着大概只有長洲人才身同感受的幽默歌詞（或投訴），如歌曲〈Just Another Day on the Ferry〉，他寫道 "Guy behind's got his knees in my back / One day I'll turn round and give him a whack / Someone is clipping his nails, it's a treat saved for the ferry so he won't have to sweep"，叫人會心微笑。

今年 67 歲的 Nick Florent，1988 年來香港教英文，剛到埗租住荃灣工業區的單位，他還記得那時經紀說附近的工廠晚上六時便下班，還不誰實情是廿四小時運作，打開窗滿是黑塵。他很快便「頂唔順」，搬到長洲山頂道，並結識現時的妻子，一住三十一年，算是長洲老街坊。早於三十年前，離島已是外國人熱門之選，Nick 當時的同事中便有不少住南丫島或長洲。他經常跟住在島上的同事三五成群一起回家，「我們最愛坐在甲板上飲啤酒，當時船上還有賣啤酒……那時未有快船，只有慢船，一個小時一班，而且我記得船上總是很擠迫和極為嘈吵。」

1919 年，港英政府為發展長洲南邊山頂為高尚住宅區頒布法令「Ordinance No.14 of 1919」，訂明任何人於南部建屋都須向政府申請，當時政府更設置了十五塊界石（boundary stone），形成一條分隔開南北的「華洋分隔線」。雖然該帶有歧視的法令於 1946 已失效，但 Nick 於 1989 年搬到長洲時，俗稱「Gweilo Ghetto」的山頂道仍主要是外國人聚居之地，當中不少是英國人，形成一個緊密的小社區，他笑言：「當我的父親來長洲參加我的婚禮時，很驚訝我們在這裡常開派對、BBQ。」他也是在山頂道的垃圾房撿到一支結他，才重拾他年輕時的興趣。但他坦言，即使住在長洲多年，自己不算十分融入島上的華人社群，直到 1991 年長洲體育館落成後，他才開始跟華人較多交集，「那時我們經常跟一個在漁民子弟學校（後改名為長洲漁會公學，現已停辦）教書的老師打羽毛球，但當時體育館無冷氣，大家都身水身汗。」

訪問當日，Nick 在他家的陽台即席獻唱一首首關於長洲和香港的歌，長洲的單車、彌敦道的人事、2019 年的漫天峰煙，都成了他歌中主題，雖然他很清楚他寫的是西方人在香港生活的體驗，但當中不少情節都能引人共鳴。值得一提的是，唱片由錄製到封面設計，都是長洲的朋友包辦，是名副其實的「長洲製造」。

BRAVO

DAY on the

Takamine

Another Day On The Ferry: A RECORD OF ISLAND LIFE

Displayed at the bar counter of Pirate Bay, a French bistro in Sai Wan, Nick's album cover features a drawing of a familiar Cheung Chau sight—a Sun Ferry coming ashore. The title *Another Day on the Ferry* makes it clear that the CD was made on Cheung Chau. His songs (or complaints) put a smile on islanders' faces. Like the lyrics of "Just Another Day on the Ferry" says:

Guy behind's got his knees in my back
One day I'll turn round and give him a whack
Someone is clipping his nails, it's a treat
Saved for the ferry so he won't have to sweep.

Nick Florent, now in his late 60s, came to Hong Kong in 1988 to teach English. When he first arrived, he rented a flat in the industrial district in Tsuen Wan. He still remembers that the agent back then claimed that the factories nearby would be closed at 6 p.m., when in fact they operated 24 hours a day and painted his windows with piling black dust. He was soon fed up and he moved to Peak Road on Cheung Chau, where he met his current wife.

Having lived on the island for over 30 years, the singer-songwriter is deeply rooted here. The outlying islands were popular locations among foreigners even three decades ago, and plenty of Nick's colleagues back then lived on Lamma Island or Cheung Chau. "We loved to sit on the deck and drink beer, when they still sold beer on the ferry," he recalls. "Back then there was no fast ferry, only the ordinary ones that ran on an hourly schedule. I remember it was always very crowded and extremely noisy on the ferry."

In 1919, the British colonial government issued the decree "Ordinance No. 14 of 1919" to develop the southern peak of Cheung Chau into a high-end residential area. It stipulated that anyone who wished to build in the southern part must obtain approval from the authorities. 15 boundary stones were thus erected to mark a dividing line between the Chinese and European populations. Though the ordinance was invalidated in 1946, by the time Nick moved to Peak Road, the neighbourhood was still known as the "Gweilo Ghetto" because it remained a small, intimate community consisting mostly of British expats. "When my father came to my wedding on Cheung Chau, he was surprised that we often held parties and barbecues here," says Nick. It was the guitar that he found at the Peak Road refuse collection point brought him back to his adolescent interest in music.

He never felt integrated into the island's Chinese community until the launch of Cheung Chau Sports Centre in 1991. It was only then that he had more interactions with the locals. "Back then we often played badminton with a teacher at the Fishermen's Children's School. The sports centre didn't have air conditioning back then, and everyone was drenched in sweat."

On the day of the interview, Nick does an impromptu performance of a song about Cheung Chau and Hong Kong on his balcony. The bicycles of Cheung Chau, the happenings on Nathan Road, and the gas-filled streets in 2019... are all featured in his songs. While Nick is aware of the fact that he is writing from a Westerner's lens, various parts of his songs still resonate with many.

From the recording to the cover, every bit of *Another Day on the Ferry* was produced by Cheung Chau friends, which is why the album is truly "made on Cheung Chau".

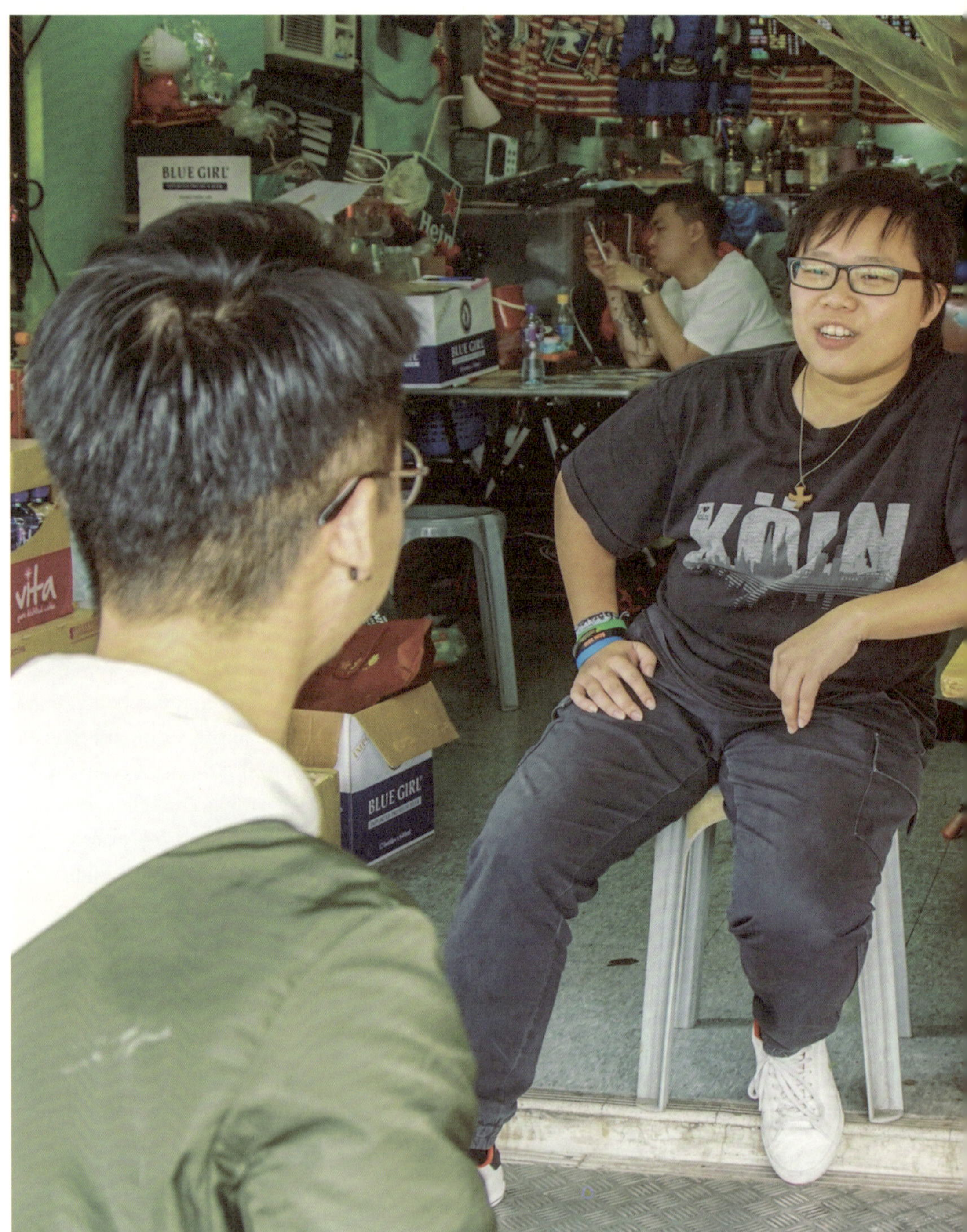
BLUE GIRL
BLUE GIRL
BLUE GIRL
vita
KÖLN

錄像創作人 Frankie

Frankie Sin

錄像創作人 Frankie
轉角士多「日泰小食」成第二個家

日泰小食，黃底紅字的招牌下掛着一隻巨型橙色魷魚公仔，兩個烤爐前放着一籃籃魷魚乾、瀨尿蝦乾、魚春等，但這些千里傳香的燒風乾海鮮卻不是這小店的賣點。

「日泰就像是我們的第二個家。」這間屹立長洲多年的士多，看似平平無奇，卻是一眾街坊的私竇。Frankie 自一八年起拍攝士多的種種，紀錄片取名為《日泰小食》，短版的英文名叫 Our Second Home，顧名思義就是導演的第二個家。訪問時老闆阿丈不在店內，熟客之一的 Frankie 一邊談，一邊自顧自取出迷彩軍綠色網布和三個 S 形掛鈎，掛在店前遮擋陽光。隔壁餐廳的姨姨打開凍櫃，取出半打啤酒，寒暄一番後把錢交給 Frankie，便回去工作。還有自稱長洲李嘉欣的霞姐，來回經過時總會停下單車，揚聲叫 Frankie 別再抽煙抽得那麼狠，「因住肺癌呀你！」Frankie 當然沒有介意關懷的咒罵，笑一笑朝她揚揚手。

Frankie 十八歲時某天，與朋友到常聚首的士多喝酒，正好友人生日，外帶了一枝酒，打算再買店家的飲料一併喝，但該士多老闆卻二話不說沒收了自攜酒。Frankie 與伙伴們氣上心頭，一怒下轉場到街角剛開業的日泰繼續把酒言歡，從此有了新的聚腳點。事隔多年，朋友們老笑他記仇，多年後仍把舊時軼事掛在嘴邊，說個樂此不疲，但正正是有如些強烈的對比，才會份外珍惜日泰的人情味。

日泰自開業以來，每天午後總會見到街坊自己搬枱搬櫈到店外的行人路上，對著大海閒聊至午夜，每張枱也堆着數打空啤酒罐。「日泰就似樹幹，而我就像爬藤。即使各有各忙的事、各有各堅守的價值，但總在給我護蔭和養份。」這份市區早已消逝的人情味，令 Frankie 想用片格留住。「沒賣小食的小食店，聚的也是沒有血緣關係的家人，哈！」他打趣小小空間的無名有實。「即使意見常有分歧，最終仍然會坐返埋一枱。」

Frankie 在長洲土生土長，2011 年赴台灣升學，本來主修油畫，後來主攻錄像創作。「畫的觀賞門檻較高，好多人會話睇唔明，而我想做出更易分享感受的作品。」一四年回來時想拍下外婆的故事。那時他總覺得自己未熟習器材，一直沒動手，但生死無常，外婆就在他生日當晚急病離世。「我第一時間趕抵醫院，但已來不及了。」憶起把他帶大的婆婆，他黯然說：「我以為她一直都會在，我真的以為她一直會在。現在滿腦子都是問題，但以後都不會有答案。」

一八年患上抑鬱症，把 Frankie 從台灣帶回長洲。「我在台灣的住處夾在巷與巷之間，沒有日光。長洲勝在夠開揚，落樓就見到街坊，可以吹下水。」他規定自己每日都要出門走走曬曬太陽，而日泰就在家樓下轉角處。他笑言：「很多時忘了器材，也可三分鐘內回家取，非常方便。」

十年人事幾番新，兒時玩伴陸續成家立室，連太平清醮也從一個超渡亡魂的習俗，變成全港的旅遊盛事。Frankie 雖會每半年回港一次，但對家鄉的記憶，卻定格在十年前離開時的模樣。格格不入的感覺令他反思：「到底什麼是思鄉？是與某些人的回憶？還是記憶中舊時的自己？」

鏡頭下看成長地，Frankie 細察當下，同時回望記憶，探討何謂思鄉，呈現家的模樣。「個人的故事可以很私密，但正因如此，才容易令人有感覺。而創作也是好私人，但藝術家就是要用作品與人交流，令人有共鳴，而不是喃喃自語。而我的這部片，就是想從個人經歷，說社會的故事，以小見大。」

「日泰是長洲的生活寫照，更是香港的縮影。不止是城鄉之別，也是不同世代的溝通。日泰滿是奇形怪狀的人，但沒有人會介意，只要你肯溝通，這兒就會歡迎你。」他頓了頓：「溝通不一定能解決問題，但至少試着了解。即使到最後難以明白，但至少我們仍可以同枱飲酒，至少我選擇連結。」

社會撕裂，無阻街坊們在日泰各抒己見，而這種彼此尊重，並不受場域規限。「本來想拍的是，這實體的家，和各人何去何從。」「但這班人，即使去到香港聚頭，仍無損連結。所以『家』這回事，就是人與人的連結。」他托托眼鏡，續說：「講完都覺得自己老土，但的確就是這樣。」

縱使島貌再變，分歧再大，長洲始終是 Frankie 的家。「每次在香港喝醉回來時，一上船就自自然放心斷片。船就是長洲人往返兩個世界的工具嘛，一上船就知道快到家啦。」

BLUE GIR

BLUE GIRL
炭業

Frankie Sin: **DOCUMENTING HIS SECOND HOME JAT TAAI SIU SIK**

Written in red characters across a yellow background is the shop name—Jat Taai Siu Sik. Two huge orange squid plushies dangle under the sign. On the trolley, baskets of dried seafood like squid, mantis shrimps, fish roe are placed in front of two grill stoves. The rich aroma of these grilled delicacies travels far and flirts with passersby on the coastline, but it is not the seafood that attracts people to the snack store.

"Jat Taai is like our second home," says Frankie, a filmmaker and a Cheung Chau native. The shop may look just like another grocery store, but it is undoubtedly the favourite hangout of many locals. Since 2018, Frankie has been filming the daily ongoings of Jat Taai, naming the documentary after the shop in Cantonese and "*Our Second Home*" in English.

Our interview at Jat Taai takes place in the absence of its store owner, who is home for an afternoon nap. And as a regular for years, Frankie knows exactly where the tables and chairs are and fishes out a camouflage fabric along with three S-shaped hooks to hang them at the storefront as a sunlight shield. A lady working at the restaurant next door comes over, opens the fridge, takes a few beers, drops some cash and heads back to work after chatting with Frankie. Another local called Ha always stops her bike whenever she passes by the shop and yells at Frankie "Beware of lung cancer!" to warn him of his heavy smoking. Of course, Frankie does not mind the harsh words as that is her way of caring for him. He just smiles and waves at her instead.

When Frankie was 18, he went to another grocery store where he usually hung out with his friends. It was his friend's birthday, and they brought their own bottle of wine and planned to buy more beverages from the store. However, the owner took their bottle away without a word. Angry and frustrated, Frankie and his friends moved to Jat Taai, a newly opened store around the corner. It became their new spot from then onwards. Many years from now, his friends still tease him for holding a grudge and repeating this old story tirelessly. But it is precisely because of this difference in attitude that makes him extra grateful for the hospitality and warmth at Jat Taai.

Locals are always seen setting tables and chairs on the street outside of Jat Taai in the afternoon. Facing the sea, they chat till midnight, with heaps of empty beer cans piling on each table. "Jat Taai is like a tree trunk and we are the vines clinging onto its branches. Each person has their own life and values, but this place always nourishes and protects us." This spirit of giving and sharing has long disappeared in urban Hong Kong, something that Frankie tries to capture through his documentary. "A snack shop , does not sell snacks, a place where people unrelated by blood bond together as a family. Ha!" Frankie is always amused by how this place is not what it appears to be. "Even though people may hold different opinions, in the end, they can all sit together at the same table."

Frankie moved to Taiwan for his studies in 2011. At first he pursued a major in painting but subsequently switched to film production. "There seems to be a threshold for appreciating paintings, as viewers always say they don't understand what they are seeing. I want to create works that can easily express my feelings."

When Frankie returned to Hong Kong in 2014, he wanted to make a film about his grandmother. He felt that he needed to hone his technical skills before he could kick-start the project. But time waits for no one. His grandmother was caught by a sudden illness and passed away overnight on the day of his birthday. "I rushed to the hospital as fast as I could, but it was already too late." His voice turns sombre when he talks about the person who raised him. "I thought she would always be there. I really thought so. I have so many questions for her, but there will never be an answer to any of them."

Frankie slipped into depression in 2018, which prompted him to move back to Cheung Chau. "My flat in Taiwan was tucked between narrow alleys. There was no sunlight there," he says. "Cheung Chau is a much more open place. You get to meet people once you step out of your door and you can always strike up a friendly chat with them." He has been forcing himself to go out daily

so that he can bathe under the sunlight. And Jat Taai happens to be right by the corner of his flat. "For so many times, I forget to bring my equipment. But I can always go home and retrieve them within three minutes. It is really convenient!" He laughs.

Times have changed. Frankie's childhood playmates are getting married and the Cheung Chau Bun Festival, a ritual to exorcise dead spirits, has become a city-wide tourist event. Though Frankie only returns to Hong Kong once every six months, his memories of his home are still frozen at what it was like ten years ago before he left for Taiwan. He always finds the changes in his hometown hard to stomach. "What does it mean to be homesick? Is it about remembering specific people? Or is it about remembering who you used to be?"

Filming the place where he grew up, Frankie observes the ongoing events on present-day Cheung Chau. Meanwhile, he examines his memories of the island, exploring what it means to miss one's homeland and finding ways to represent the idea of home.

"Personal stories can be very intimate and because of this, they can easily evoke emotion." Creative expressions can too be highly personal, he says, but artists should not only talk about themselves. "We should create moments of exchange and resonance with others through our works. In this documentary, I would like to talk about the stories of the community through my own experiences. In so doing, I will be able to approach broader subjects through the small moments in life."

"Jat Taai is a mirror of people's lives on Cheung Chau. It is also representative of our lives in Hong Kong. It is not about the difference between living in the suburbs or living in the city, or how different generations can communicate with each other. Jat Taai is full of strange people, yet nobody bats an eye. As long as you are willing to communicate, this place welcomes you."

"Communication may not solve all the problems, but at least we can try to understand each other. Even if we can't understand each other in the end, we can still sit at the same table and drink together. At least we choose to connect with each other."

Despite polarising social conflicts in recent years, locals continue to share their views while respecting each other's opinions. And such liberty should not only be available at Jat Taai. "Originally I wanted to film Jat Taai as our home and what happened to the people there. But our bond is still strong even when we gather in the city. Perhaps the concept of home is about the connection between each other." He continues, "I know this sounds old-fashioned, but this is how it is."

No matter how the island of Cheung Chau transforms or how different opinions set people apart, this place is still Frankie's home. "Every time I come home after getting drunk in Hong Kong, I can relax and let my mind wander on its own once I board the ferry. Once I get on, I know I will be home soon."

島人源
ISLAND ORIGIN
CHEUNG CHAU, HONG KONG
PATRON OF OUR ISLAND
VISA
島人源
ISLAND ORIGIN
CHEUNG CHAU, HONG KONG
文創工坊
culture
creative
workshop
DOOR OPEN
DOOR OPEN
MASK
WELCOME
長洲
源創
島嶼特色文創紀念品
Island Culture Creative Products

島人源

Island Origin

島人源原創 T-shirt
長洲手信不只有平安包

手信的意義在於呈現一個地方的文化和特色，給人留念。但縱觀長洲的手信舖，賣的不外乎是平安包造型的精品，或是手繩、貝殼等充滿東南亞風味的飾物，十年如一。然而，真正的長洲特色，不只是平安包和海光與海灘的小島印象。在北社街的島人源店主阿西，就以自家製的 T-shirt，呈現鮮為人知的長洲故事和傳統文化，譬如其中一件繪上兩個威武的男子，原來是救生員：「長洲的救生員在拯溺界非常有名，由於他們是在海上受訓，較熟水性，而且現時泳灘常用的救生筏也是長洲率先採用。」T-shirt 上的救生員化身風神和雷神，非常威風，足見阿西對他們的敬意。

從事廣告的阿西是長洲人，但小學後便到市區居住，後來到上海工作十多年，直至 2017 年搬回長洲，他說得淡然：「人到了某個年紀，想慢下來。」雖然離開長洲十多年，但其實他與長洲的連繫從未間斷，每年太平清醮，他都會回到長洲，拆包山、推車巡遊、飄色等他都落手落腳幫忙，他回憶道：「太平清醮是連繫整個社區的活動，打醮前三晚這裡很熱鬧，很多人在東堤燒烤、飲啤酒，但大家都嚴守齋戒，就算是大隻佬都是燒瓜瓜菜菜，晚上其他社團的舞麒麟會過來打招呼，熱鬧過新年……打醮就好像是三日之內，動員一萬幾千人去『發癲』，除長洲之外，哪裡可以做到？」

雖然太平清醮是長洲人團聚的大日子，但阿西強調，打醮不是嘉年華，它是為神而出現的，「人們來到我的店，問我有冇平安包圖案 T-shirt，但我說太平清醮的重點是四個神祇，不是平安包。」他的產品也有四個大神，分別是北帝、山神、土地和大士王，但阿西特意以簡約的線條繪畫四神，令原本殺氣騰騰的神明變得平易近人。

在長洲開小店，成本較市區低，但運輸成本較高，平日人流亦不多，阿西形容長洲是「修羅場」，「無論開什麼店，都一定要有『撚手嘢』，否則混不下去。」島人源的定位清晰，吸引不少有心探索長洲的遊客，「北社街是老街，來店的客人通常都是喜歡深度一點去認識一個地方，探索新事物的人。」

阿西開店前，亦花了不少時間去做資料搜集，惡補小島的歷史和文化，在他眼中，長洲是香港的縮影，「長洲幾百年前已經是一個熱鬧的墟市，澳門或其他地方的船會到長洲補給，如同香港作為移民城市，流動性很高，很多來自不同城市的人聚居。」他又指，長洲是漁民社會，而某程度上，漁民精神也是香港精神的縮影：刻苦、安份、重視傳統、樂觀、勇於挑戰。而阿西也漸漸沾染了島民的豁達：「水上人出海睇天做人，他們總喜歡說：『係咁㗎啦！』，即使今日大風大浪，但總相信明天會放晴，就好像在長洲開店，不會日日都很多客人，但『係咁㗎啦！』」

從阿西的口吻，聽得出他對長洲的喜愛，他常說：「香港人經常嫌棄自己本土的東西，但如果人們有空時去興記（位於觀音灣的士多）看看海，飲枝啤酒，你會發覺原來香港可以這麼美，這麼寫意，無需要去日本或出國……你別看它這麼小的一個島，但它不就是香港人所追求的理想生活嗎？」

ISLAND ORIGIN

島人源
ISLAND ORIGIN
100%cotton
Designed in Hong Kong
Made in China

ISLAND ORIGIN
WELCOME TO ISLAND ORIGIN

海上衛士勝龍圖
夜光貼紙
Neon color Stickers

Island Origin: **ALTERNATIVE SOUVENIRS FROM CHEUNG CHAU**

Souvenirs are made to represent the culture and characteristics of a place, to serve as mementos for visitors. Most of the souvenir shops on Cheung Chau offer Ping On bun accessories, braided bracelets, seashells or other jewellery items with a Southeast Asian twist. There are not many other variations even after ten years.

But Cheung Chau is not only about these typical impressions of island life like the sun and the beach. Ah Sai, owner of Island Origin located on Pak She Street, creates original T-shirts that represent the traditional cultures and stories of Cheung Chau. For instance, the two ferocious-looking men depicted on one of the T-shirts are lifeguards. “Lifeguards from Cheung Chau are well-known among other rescuers. They are trained in the sea and can swim very well. The life rafts we often use on beaches nowadays were first introduced on Cheung Chau.” Powerful and strong, the lifeguards were depicted as the God of Wind and the God of Thunder in a show of respect from Ah Sai.

Now in the advertising industry, Ah Sai was born and raised on Cheung Chau. He moved to the city after primary school and went to Shanghai for work for almost ten years. Ah Sai only moved back to Cheung Chau in 2017. “When you are at a certain age, you would like to slow down a bit.”

He may have left Cheung Chau for more than a decade, but his bond with his birthplace remains strong. He always returns for the Bun Festival every year. Dismantling bun towers, pushing the parade cars, and helping out at the Piu Sik Parade, Ah Sai is not afraid of getting his hands dirty.

“The Bun Festival is an activity that connects the whole community. Three nights before Da Jiu, the island would be bustling with activities, with locals barbequing and drinking beer on the east bay. And we all respect the ritual of going vegetarian, even the buff guys only barbeque greens and squashes. The qilin dance visits every shop for greetings. Da Jiu lasts around three days, and it is as if we organise thousands of people to celebrate and go crazy. This is not something you can easily do elsewhere.”

The Cheung Chau Bun Festival indeed is a big day for locals to gather together, but Ah Sai stresses that Da Jiao is not a carnival, it is for the gods. “When tourists ask if I have a T-shirt with Ping On buns printed on it, I told them, ‘The Cheung Chau Bun Festival is about celebrating the four deities, not the Ping On buns.’” His products feature the four deities, namely Pak Tai, the God of Mountains, the God of Soil and Ground, and the King of All Spirits (Tai Shi Wong). By using simple lines to illustrate them, the fearsome gods look more approachable and friendly.

While the overall costs for operating an independent shop on Cheung Chau are less than that in the city, the transportation costs are much higher and there is far less daily footfall. Ah Sai describes Cheung Chau as a "shuraba": "No matter what kind of shop you are opening, you must have a certain specialty, or else it will be hard to stay in business." Island Origin has a clear brand positioning and can attract many tourists who are interested in learning more about Cheung Chau. "Pak She Street is an old street. Most of the customers who come into my shop want to know more about the place in an in-depth way. They are the kind that loves to explore new things."

Prior to launching Island Origin, Ah Sai had spent a lot of time researching the history and culture of the island. In his eyes, Cheung Chau is a miniature of Hong Kong. "Hundreds of years ago, Cheung Chau was a lively city. Boats from Macau or other places would stop at Cheung Chau to replenish their supplies. Similarly, Hong Kong, as a city of migrants, has experienced a lot of movements. People from other cities have moved to live here."

Cheung Chau is a society of fishermen, and the spirit of the fishermen to a large extent resembles that of Hong Kong—hardworking, law-abiding, tradition-centric, optimistic, and keen to embrace challenges. As time passes, Ah Sai too is influenced by the optimistic attitude of fellow islanders. "As people who live by the sea, their lives are dependent on the weather conditions of the day," he says. "They always say, 'Well, that's that!' Even when they face strong winds and mounting waves, they always trust that the sun will come out the next day. It is just like opening a shop on Cheung Chau, you won't have many customers every day, but 'well, that's that!'"

Ah Sai's passion for Cheung Chau always comes through in the way he speaks. "Hongkongers always despise things from their own city. If they have the time to visit Hing Kee [a beach bar in Kwun Yam Wan] and have a beer by the sea, you will find Hong Kong a beautiful place too. It is such a relaxing place, and you don't need to go to Japan or overseas."

"Don't look down on such a small island. Isn't it the perfect life that every Hongkonger is looking for?"

島中坊研

Island Workbench

島中坊研
長洲製造的手作工藝

長洲土生土長的 Amy 和 Steven 同讀設計出身，2014 年創立自家手作品牌，名為「島中坊研」。

「官方解釋是『在小島中的工作坊研究』，但其實也是想取《稻中乒團》的諧音。」Amy 怡然自得地打趣。有誰想過如此清新簡約的品牌，背後原來隱隱向爆笑漫畫致意。

Amy 和 Steven 本來各有全職，修讀服裝設計的 Amy 為一間國際衣飾公司設計毛衣，朝九晚六的安逸生活卻令她萌生另闖天地的念頭。「當時工作模式好死板，每年兩季只需交出一二百個設計，整個流程又乏味，沒有太多機會發揮創意，而我想建立一些屬於自己的東西，便試試開設自己的品牌。」

芸芸自家設計的產品中，不乏獨特的長洲小島色彩，當中手織魚網袋更是為延續傳統工藝而生。六七十年代，不論老幼都會穿塑膠花、剪線頭幫補家計，長洲人也不例外。「一打開門，就見八個十個姨姨在踩衣車趕工。」舊時沒有膠袋，島上婦女便活用鉤織魚網的技術，製作買菜袋，還吸引了男生學習織造，以賺取零用。Amy 媽媽是在家中作業的紡織高手，自小耳濡目染下，萌生濃厚興趣，選科時就填了時裝設計。

時移勢易，眼看紡織製衣漸成夕陽工業，Amy 不忍前人高超手藝就此浪費，便把傳統技藝與文化脈絡融入設計。她舉着金銀交替的手織漁網袋說：「水上人喜歡買金保值，所以我便想用這個選色去呼應他們的習俗。而其他魚網袋設計同樣只會調整大小和物料，盡量保留舊日的風味。」他們又找退休漁民出山幫忙編織。從構思到製作，全出自長洲島民之手，真正長洲製造。

Amy 和 Steven 從網店做起，漸漸累積一批知音熟客，而一次在賽馬會創意藝術中心的定期手作市集，令他們思索起品牌和自己的未來。「第一次參與市集，真是大開眼界，拓闊了我們對維生模式的想像。」攤檔放着三款設計，沒有現貨，只接訂單，但反應之好完全超乎預料，為二人注下強心針。他們於是決定要放手一搏，雙雙辭去在市區的工作，回到出生地開店。

Amy 想起那年赤手空拳創業的無懼：「那時只是二十出頭，沒什麼包袱家累，即使不行，就重回打工仔行列，也沒什麼大不了啦。」

首間實體店選址鄰近東灣，除了出售自家手作，還兼賣其他本地品牌的文創精品。生意漸上軌道後，需另找存放和製作空間，便於 2017 年中在天后廟附近開設「樹下店」。店舖前方供應輕食和自製飲料，後方則立着一匹匹布料和疊滿多盒配件，為 Amy 和 Steven 研究和製作的工場。

Amy 現已是兩家實體店的主持人，剛為人母的她還會通宵達旦趕製訂單。「好忙，不停分身真的好忙，但能全身投入值得的人和事，又真的沒什麼好抱怨呢。」笑容和煦的她是如此滿足。

SALE

OBSCURA

Island Workbench: **REFASHIONING FISHERMEN'S HERITAGE**

Cheung Chau natives Amy and Steven both studied design before launching their handmade brand Island Workbench in 2014. "The official explanation [of the name] is 'a workshop's research on an island', but we also wanted it to be slightly homophonic with the Chinese translated title of *The Ping Pong Club*," Amy explains. Who would have thought that the name of this minimalist brand is a nod to the perverted comedy?

Amy, a fashion design graduate, used to design knitwear for an international clothing and accessories company. The stable nine-to-six work hours, however, prompted her to explore a different way of living. "Back then, the mode of working was very fixed and rigid, you just needed to submit 100 to 200 designs across two seasons each year," she says. "The entire process was boring and had little room for creativity. I wanted to build something that belonged to myself, so I gave it a try and launched my brand."

Many of their products draw on the unique characteristics of Cheung Chau, particularly the Fish Net Bag which was created in the hope of passing on the traditional craft. During the 60s and 70s, the old and young in the city would contribute to their families' income by assembling plastic flowers and doing needlework, and Cheung Chau islanders were no different. "You would find eight to ten aunties completing rush orders on their sewing machines in a single flat," Amy recalls.

That was a time before the prevalence of plastic bags. Many women on the island would crochet grocery bags with fishnet-making techniques. Boys would also pick up the skills to earn some pocket money. Amy had developed a deep interest in textiles under the influence of her mother, who was skilled in knitting and crocheting. Naturally, she chose to major in fashion design.

The golden days of the fish-net knitting have long been over, but Amy did not want to see the end of such precious technical skills. She thus incorporated traditional craftsmanship and cultural contexts into her designs. Holding a handmade gold and silver Fish Net Bag, she says: "Boat people like to buy gold as a way to hedge their fortunes, so I wanted to use this colour pairing to echo this custom. Like other Fish Net Bags, I am only adjusting the size and material, keeping it as original as possible." The brand also invites the retired fishing community to help with the production. From concept to production, the bags are all "made on Cheung Chau" as they are born from the hands of the islanders.

Amy and Steven started with an online shop, which allowed them to slowly build an appreciative clientele. And one experience at the regular handicraft fair at Jockey Club Creative Arts Centre prompted them to rethink the development of the brand and their future. "It was an eye-opening experience as it was our first time joining a bazaar, which expanded our imagination of how one could make a living." With only three designs showcasing at their stall, none of them was available for sale on the spot. But visitors were enthusiastic in placing pre-orders, which hugely boosted Amy and Steven's confidence. They finally decided to go all out by quitting their full-time jobs and returning to their birthplace to open a brick-and-mortar store.

Amy says that they could start a business from scratch because they were fearless. "We were in our early 20s and didn't have too many cares and woes. Even if it couldn't work out, we would just look for jobs again. It's not such a big deal." They chose to open their first shop near Tung Wan, selling their own products as well as merchandise from other local brands.

As the business grew, they had to look for a bigger storage and studio space, hence the launch of the "Under the Tree" branch near Tin Hau Temple in mid-2017. The shopfront served light meals and homemade beverages, while the back of the store functions as their studio, filled with piles of fabrics and boxes of accessories.

As an owner of two stores, and now a mom, Amy often needs to work overnight to complete the orders. "It's been so busy, wearing multiple hats and such," she says with a warm smile. "But being able to fully invest in something worthwhile, there really isn't anything I should be complaining about."

占與Chunk

Chunk

占與CHUNK
屬於海和天的藍色小肥人

他生活在海邊，藍皮膚，肥嘟嘟，一頭捲髮，閒來無事最喜歡坐在海邊望海，飲醉酒便倒頭大睡，摺起的肚皮隨呼吸一上一下，眼皮不自覺半開半合……他是搪膠公仔 Chunk，Jim 是他的創作者。

Jim 在長洲長大，父母在長洲經營雜貨店，成長時期大部分時間在島，與山和天作伴。大學修讀平面設計，畢業後曾於潮流雜誌任職攝影師，受同事薰陶，開始接觸 figure 公仔，後來轉到一間玩具製作公司工作，並開始設計和創作自己的角色。

Chunk 的造型和性格源於 Jim 的生活：他的肥胖身型和捲髮，依據他一位朋友的外貌特徵；他的藍，是 Jim 經常接觸到的天空和海洋；他的 chill，來自島上生活的率性隨意。不論是長期笑咪咪露出兔仔牙的 Baby Chunk，還是飲醉酒就訓到流口水的肥大叔 Chunk，總是一副悠然自得的樣子。訪問時 Jim 邊吃着 all-day breakfast 邊說：「他性格佗佻，懶洋洋。他提醒人們，累的時候可以放鬆一下，不一定要無時無刻積極認真。希望大家見到佢，有種：『嘩！原來生活可以咁舒服！』的感覺。」

Chunk 受到不少外國人喜愛，Jim 亦希望借這個角色，令人認識到長洲這地方。例如幾年前他曾結合 Chunk 和平安包，但卻不會專門造個平安包版本去售賣，他強調：「長洲已經很商業化，我不想再消費這個地方，只是讓人知道有這個小島便夠了。」

Jim 的童年，不外乎是上山下海這些島民眼中很平常的事，又或者在北帝廟外的扶手瀡滑梯。他說他成長時已錯過了長洲最好玩的日子：「我聽說以前長洲的海邊籃球場很多人去玩遙控車，玩到出晒煙嗰種！後來又有很多人在那裏踩板，周末晚上總有七、八十人，很多外面的滑板愛好者會專誠到長洲搞比賽。」現時該球場仍是島上板仔板女的「蒲點」，但盛況不如前。想不到這離市區最遠的小島，曾經是次文化重地！

不少與 Jim 同齡的朋友都因讀書或結婚搬到市區，但 Jim 沒有搬離過長洲，即使現時每日需花幾個小時到市區上班，「我沒有特別嚮往市區生活，習慣了長洲的生活，可以很即興，晚上食飽飯無事做，打個電話可以去朋友家，十五分鐘就見到面，不用刻意去約。」縱使每日下班回來吃個飯已是晚上十點，但他不介意這種「不方便」：「長洲係我屋企，落船踏出碼頭的一刻，我已經有種『回到家了』的感覺。相反在市區，即使回到家也聽到外面嘈雜的車聲，精神上難以 relax。」他記得曾到東南亞的海島旅行，聽到舢舨的「噗噗」聲、渡輪的響咹聲，他赫然發覺：「這是長洲的聲音。」是家的聲音。

Chunk: **JIM'S CHUBBY BLUE FRIEND**

He lives by the sea and has blue skin. He is chubby and his hair is curly. He loves to sit by the seaside and stare out into the ocean when he has nothing to do. He dozes off when he is drunk, with the folds of his belly rising and falling as he breathes...

His name is Chunk, a vinyl figure. And Jim is his creator.

Jim grew up on Cheung Chau, where his parents ran a grocery store. Most of his childhood was spent living by the sea, the mountains and the sky. Upon completing his studies in graphic design, Jim worked as a photographer for a fashion magazine where his colleagues introduced him to toy figures. Soon after, he joined a toy manufacturing company and started designing and creating his characters.

Chunk's outlook and personalities are inspired by Jim's daily experiences. His bulky physique and curls are all characteristics of a friend of Jim's; his blue skin tone is drawn from the colours of the sky and the ocean; his laid-back character is found in the carefree lifestyle of Cheung Chau.

Be it Baby Chunk whose front teeth always peaks out when he smiles or chubby Uncle Chunk who drools when he sleeps after a few drinks, they all look so at peace with themselves. "Chunk is quite lazy and always takes it easy. He is there to remind people that you can chill a bit when you are tired." Jim says as he enjoys his all-day breakfast, "You don't always have to be so serious. I hope people will think 'Oh! I too can live a breezy life!' whenever they see him."

Chunk is also well-loved by audiences abroad. Jim hopes that more people can learn of Cheung Chau through Chunk. Jim tried creating a Ping On bun version of Chunk but refused to manufacture it for sale. "Cheung Chau has already been highly commercialised. I don't want to make a profit out of this place in that way. As long as people get to know about here, I'm happy."

Jim spent his childhood hiking or swimming in the ocean or sliding down the handrails of the Pak Tai Temple—common activities amongst fellow islanders. Yet he still thinks he missed the most exciting experiences of the Cheung Chau kids. "I heard that a lot of people went to the basketball court by the seaside back then to play with remote-controlled cars. The kind that had smoke coming out of it!"

"After that, a lot of skateboarders went there, around 70 to 80 of them every night during weekends. Skateboarders elsewhere would come all the way to Cheung Chau to hold skateboarding competitions." Nobody could have thought that an island miles away from the city was a vital hub for subculture.

Many friends who are the same age as Jim have moved out to the city for their studies or after they got married. However, Jim never leaves Cheung Chau even though it still takes him a few hours to commute every day. "I am not that fond of living in the city. I am too used to living on Cheung Chau," he says. "Everything can be very spontaneous. If there is nothing to do after dinner, you can phone your friends and hang out with them. It only takes 15 minutes for us to see each other. You don't need to make plans."

"Cheung Chau is my home. The second I step out of the pier, I already have a feeling of 'Ah, I'm home!' It is very different from living in the city, where I can still hear the noises from the cars even at home. I just can't relax." He still remembers his trip to the archipelagos in Southeast Asia. When he heard the engine sounds from sampans or the horns from ferries, he came to a sudden realisation: "This is the sound of Cheung Chau."

And that is the sound of home.

渡日書店

TO-DAY BOOKSTORE

渡日書店
書到伴過日子時

「終於唔使出香港買書啦！」2021 年初秋，渡日書店正式開業，不少路過的、特地到訪的街坊如是說。

其實在此之前，長洲也曾有買書的地方。有外籍街坊經營過英文二手書店，但現已結業。現址街市對面的長洲書店也曾賣過金庸、亦舒等流行小說，但早已轉型，銷售文儀用品。渡日書店的開張，令這個離島區中人煙最稠密的島嶼，終於再有書店。

渡日由七位街坊朋友合資開辦，其誕生可謂由無數緣份組成，而交織的契機就是長洲。店主之一的阿嬋說：「要不是搬了進來，就唔會認識呢班人，亦都唔會有這間書店，成件事也可算因長洲而生。」開店所需資金由七人攤分，她表示：「每人夾少少，跟夾租個 studio（工作室）差不多，唔會太大負擔。在長洲尚可做到唔賺唔蝕，換成在市區就諗都唔洗諗。」所以說，沒有長洲，就沒有渡日。

在長洲開書店的念頭，萌生自數年前聯乘四個離島的「船到橋頭生活節」，阿嬋想過開放家中天台，和朋友一起辦一個快閃圖書館。雖然最終未有成事，但他們相信總有其他島民對閱讀和書本有需求。阿嬋說：「長洲咁大個島，點可以無書店㗎？」這班街坊相聚時常會聊起這個想法，但一直沒刻意張羅，直至某夜飯後路過，看到米黃色鐵閘上掛着招租告示，便聯絡業主。另一位店主 Damon 說：「若要搵地產的話，首先要知自己想要什麼，但我們根本沒計劃過要入幾多本書，或規模如何。一切都是見到這個空間，才有了實質想像。」加上地舖位於北社街與國民路交界、距離東灣海灘只有兩三分鐘，不乏街坊遊客經過，毋須費勁吸引人流。

空間有限，渡日的選書貴精不貴多，主要是文史哲、繪本、藝術書、獨立小誌。店中央的「豬肉枱」每隔幾個月便會轉新主題。首個主題「植物世界」，源於各店主對種植的興趣，家中也有相關書籍。第三個主題「亂世 活好」是因正值農曆新年和疫情肆虐，想介紹一些能帶來力量的書目，如一行禪師的著作，希望讀者能在字裡行間稍稍紓懷。阿嬋相信：「我們所關心的議題，也會與大眾重疊。」

長洲多人看書嗎？阿嬋坦言並非大多數，尤其網絡上充斥着各類即時資訊。「但閱讀可以帶我們進入另一個時空。兵荒馬亂時更加要讀書，幫到自己思考更多。」她舉例，小說《非關命運》圍繞納粹集中營，看似歷史久遠的題材，其實可以引導我們深刻反省現世的事。開店至今，閱讀成了不少街坊和店主們的共同話題。有街坊表示，因渡日而重拾看實體書的習慣。又有街坊每星期會選購兩本書，即使家中的書未看完，也會用實際行動定期支持。

七位朋友的共識，是想辦一間「親民啲、家庭式」的社區書店。渡日兼售香港製造的生活雜貨，如悅和豉油、喵坊廁紙、原居文化的酒釀，也試過團購梅窩農夫的有機菜，全是店長們自己會回購的產品。除了「自肥」，他們也想把本地製作介紹給更多街坊，推廣環保和在地消費等理念。阿嬋和 Damon 認為，書就如柴米油鹽一樣同屬生活所需，不比其他貨品高尚。

店舖面積雖只得約二百呎，但沒有堆滿書籍雜貨，反而騰空出樓梯底的空間，鋪了地毯置了咕𠺢，供大大小小讀者盤坐打書釘。外間轉變速度之快，常叫人措手不及，而渡日就是想成為一個能讓來客休息散心的空間。不久前某個氣氛低沉的日子，有位姨姨看過新聞後便遠道從沙田過來，為的只是翻翻書、抖抖氣。

營運半年，兩位店主直言，他們仍舊不設任何業績指標。Damon 的父親營商，反而令他早自知不懂圖利，即使現在經營書店，推薦時只會說真實感想，不懂推銷，引來其他店長笑他「倒米」。Damon 表示：「買書是一種會投入情感的消費，不可能純粹在商言商。」太著眼利潤的話，反而會令書店變質。

開店以來唯一稍作調整的，只有對自己的要求。阿嬋說：「開店前本來只當是一個朋友 project，沒有什麼期盼。但漸漸從外界的提醒、客人的期望，意識到書店的角色，會反思如何用不同的姿態與社會連結。」當俄羅斯入侵烏克蘭後，她便積極入手東歐現代史的相關讀物，透過選書回應時代。

對於渡日的未來，阿嬋貫徹開店以來的心態：「隨緣啦。」Damon 意見一致，說：「見步行步吧。」這班街坊，相信一切隨遇而安，只望能在所愛的小島守住一片空間，好好同渡每一日。

法律是什麼?
人的條件
真理的史詩

TO-DAY BOOKSTORE: **WHEN YOU NEED A BREATHER, READ**

"Finally! I don't have to go to the city to buy books anymore!" Locals cheered when they passed by TO-DAY BOOKSTORE on its official opening day in the early autumn of 2021.

Cheung Chau used to have other locations that sold books. Once an expat resident had opened a second-hand bookstore for English titles, but that shut a few years ago. The Cheung Chau Bookstore opposite the wet market sold popular fiction by authors such as Jin Yong and Isabel Nee, but it has long since switched to selling stationery products. With the opening of TO-DAY BOOKSTORE, Hong Kong's most populous outlying island finally has a bookshop again.

TO-DAY BOOKSTORE, a joint venture by seven friends, would not have been possible without a series of serendipities on Cheung Chau. "If I hadn't moved here, I wouldn't have met this group of friends, and this bookstore wouldn't have come to life," Sim, one of the owners says. "So you could say that the whole thing was born out of Cheung Chau."

Operating expenses such as rent are split between the seven friends. "Since everyone chips in a little, it is like renting a studio without causing too much of a burden," Sim says. "It is still possible to break even on Cheung Chau, whereas this would be unthinkable in the city." That is why it's fair to say that TO-DAY BOOKSTORE would not have existed without Cheung Chau.

The idea of opening a bookstore on Cheung Chau first took shape several years ago thanks to the Inter-Island Festival, which featured the connections between Peng Chau, Mui Wo, Chi Ma Wan, and Cheung Chau. Sim thought of launching a pop-up library with some friends on the rooftop of her home for the art festival. Though it did not work out in the end, they believed that there must be other islanders who enjoy reading and having easy access to books as much as they do.

"How can such a big island like Cheung Chau not have a bookstore?" Sim questions.

This group of friends always brought up the idea whenever they got together, but never acted on it until one evening, they spotted after dinner a rental notice hanging on a newly painted cream-coloured iron gate. They then contacted the landlord.

"If we were to look for a property, we must first know what we were looking for, but we never had planned for the number of books to be stocked," says Damon, another owner. "It was only after seeing this space that we were able to start imagining how it would be." The shop is situated at the intersection of Pak She Street and Kwok Man Road, only a few minutes away from Tung Wan Beach. There is no lack of locals and tourists passing by, hence no need to spare efforts to attract foot traffic.

TO-DAY BOOKSTORE prioritises quality over quantity when it comes to book selection, specialising in literature, history, philosophy, picture books, art books, and independent zines. The table at the centre of the shop switches themes every other few months. The first theme, "The World of Plants," comes from the owners' collective interests in gardening, as well as related titles at their homes. The third theme "Live Well Amid Turbulent Times" strives to share some invigorating books, such as titles by Thich Nhat Hanh, at the time of the Lunar New Year and the height of the fifth wave of the COVID-19 pandemic. "The topics that we care about would also overlap with those of the public," Sim says. They always hope that readers can find some solace between the lines.

Are there many book lovers on Cheung Chau? "Not the majority," Sim confesses. Especially when there are all sorts

of instant information available on the internet, she adds. "But then reading can transport us to another time and space. It's all the more helpful to read in times of chaos, to help you think more." She uses the novel *Fatelessness* as an example, which revolves around a Nazi concentration camp. The topic may seem to be something from a distant past, but it can lead us to reflect deeply on our times.

Since the opening of the shop, reading has become a shared topic among locals. Some say that they have started reading physical books again thanks to TO-DAY BOOKSTORE. One regular always buys two books every week as a show of support, even though he may not have finished reading his previous purchases.

The seven friends came to a consensus to start a community bookstore that is approachable and family-friendly. TO-DAY BOOKSTORE sells groceries that are made in Hong Kong, such as Yuet Wo soy sauce, Mil Mill recycled toilet rolls and organic produce from Mui Wo farmers. All these products are ones that the shop owners would repurchase over and over again for themselves as well. And these groceries are part of our daily necessities like books, which are in no way superior to other commodities.

Though the store is only about 200 sq. ft in size, it is not cluttered with books and groceries. Instead, the space under the stairs has been cleared out and carpeted for readers of all ages to sit comfortably with their noses in books. The world changes at such a speed that people are often caught off guard, so TO-DAY BOOKSTORE aims to provide a space where visitors can relax and take a break. On a gloomy day not long ago, a granny came over all the way from Sha Tin, just to flip some books and catch a breather after reading the news.

Even after operating for half a year, the two owners still have not set any performance indicators. Damon's father is a businessman and that has ironically led him realise early on that he knows nothing about profit-making. Even now, whenever he recommends books at the shop, he always only expresses his opinions truthfully. "Book business is a sort of emotional purchase, it can't purely be about money." Focusing too much on profit may risk changing the nature of the bookstore, he adds.

The only slight adjustment since the shop's launch is the owners' expectations for themselves. "Before opening, I just thought of it as a friends' project and did not set any expectations," Sim says. "However, I have come to realise the role of a bookshop from customers' expectations and reflect on how we can connect with the community in different ways." Russia's invasion of Ukraine has propelled her to stock titles related to the modern history of Eastern Europe, responding to the times through book selection.

As for the future of TO-DAY BOOKSTORE, Sim maintains the same "go with the flow" mentality since the birth of the store, to which Damon agrees: "We move forward step by step." This group of friends believes that everything will follow its course. They only wish to have each day be a day well-spent on the island they love.

後記

零三年沙士爆發，全港十八區均錄得個案，唯長洲例外。不過，大圍環境不景氣下，東堤小築發生連串燒炭事件，令長洲蒙上自殺勝地之名，令人聞島喪膽。為了重振本土旅遊業，港府在零五年批准恢復停辦了二十七年的午夜搶包山，並大力推動太平清醮這個特色節慶。雖能一洗島上蕭條，但亦對居民的出入和生活構成不便。新冠疫情下無法外遊，每逢假期週末更加人頭湧湧，比市區的人流更多。

但長洲從來都不只是一個旅遊熱點。

長洲的過去與現在，也是香港近代史的縮影。經歷過開埠初期的華洋分割，二次大戰後長洲同樣百廢待興。一向以海為家、以水為生的長洲，見證五十年代輕工業、漁業的興盛，住屋、水電、醫療等民生需要得以逐步改善。八十年代製造業主導時期走向尾聲，改由旅遊業等服務業主導，傳統手藝漸漸式微，面臨失傳。

特此感謝每位願意與我們詳談的受訪者，還有不吝細訴小島一點一滴的每一位街坊。當中不乏三代相傳的祖業，也有選擇在此扎根營生的新島民。他們所嚮往的、所投入的或有不同，有人竭力承傳，有人不斷創新，更多人相信兩者相輔相成，同樣視長洲、香港為家。

此書結集於瘟疫蔓延時，過程中有些商號已結業、有些受訪者已離港，猶幸我們能摘錄他們的故事，略略記下點點小島風光。

Afterword

When SARS broke out in 2003, cases were recorded across Hong Kong, except for Cheung Chau. However, the ensuing socialeconomic slump led to a series of charcoal-burning suicides at the island's holiday resorts, hence the reputation of a suicide hotspot that terrified many at the mention of its name.

In a bid to boost tourism, the government brought back in 2005 the midnight bun scrambling contest, which had previously been suspended for 27 years, to make the Cheung Chau Bun Festival a local and international highlight. The tourists and festivity have no doubt dispelled the bleakness, but at the expense of the islanders. In 2022 when overseas travel remained largely banned under lockdown restrictions, outlying islands such as Cheung Chau were flooded by streams of urban dwellers every weekend.

But Cheung Chau is never just a tourist spot.

Cheung Chau's past and present are also a microcosm of Hong Kong's modern history. Upon experiencing a period of segregation of the Westerners and Chinese locals in the early colonial years, Cheung Chau—much like the rest of Hong Kong—was also left in a state of ruins after World War II. The Cheung Chau that had always lived by and relied on the sea harvested the prosperity of the light industry and fishery in the 1950s, as well as the gradual improvement of essential facilities such as housing, electricity, and medicine. In the 80s, the industrial-led era came to an end, only to be replaced by a surge of service industries such as tourism. Traditional craftsmanship has since been at risk of vanishing and becoming a rarity.

Our sincerest gratitude to all the interviewees and locals who have generously shared their stories with us. Among them are many traditional businesses that have been passed down through generations, as well as a number of new islanders who have chosen to start a life here. Some are trying their best to keep traditions alive, while others strive to break boundaries and create possibilities. More often these two visions complement one another, as they both regard Cheung Chau and Hong Kong as their home.

This book was compiled at the height of the COVID-19 pandemic, during which some businesses have shut and some interviewees have left Hong Kong. We consider ourselves most fortunate to have been able to pen their stories and capture bits and pieces of Cheung Chau in this book.

策劃及出版 Conceptualised and published by
Nous

共同策劃 Co-presented by
FOSA

撰文 Authors
何光 Sim Ho
余知樂 Swimmie Yu

中文編輯 Chinese Editor
何光 Sim Ho

英文編輯 English Editor
余知樂 Swimmie Yu

攝影 Photography
張才生 Samson Cheung

翻譯 Translation
Narratives Studio

設計指導 Design Direction
Nous

書籍設計 Book Design
麥晉軒 Ken Mak

插畫 Illustration
黃卓瑩 Wing Huang

印刷 Printing
高行印刷有限公司 Colham Printing Co Ltd

贊助 Sponsored by
西園農莊管理有限公司
Sai Yuen Farm Management Company Limited

發行 Distributed by
一代匯集
Generation Collection
九龍旺角塘尾道 64 號龍駒企業大廈 10 樓 B&D 室
Flat B&D, 10/F, Lucky Horse Industrial Bldg, 64 Tong Mei Road, Kln, H.K.
電話 Tel: 852-27838102/ 93114122
傳真 Fax: 852-23960050/ 852-27821529
電郵 E-mail: gcdick@biznetvigator.com

First Edition: October 2024
2024 年 10 月初版

ISBN: 978-988-70780-0-5